Resisting Gossip

Winning the War of the Wagging Tongue

Matthew C. Mitchell

CLC PUBLICATIONS

Fort Washington, PA 19034

In Praise of *Resisting Gossip*

"With clarity and the precision of a spiritual physician, Matt cuts deep into the cancerous disease that produces words that hurt and defame. Not only will this book help you keep your tongue in check, but it will also be a helpful navigational tool in guiding your speech toward the joyful discipline of using words to help and heal others to the glory of God! Put the principles of this book into practice, and you, your family, friends and colleagues will all be better off!"

—**Dr. Joseph M. Stowell**,
president of Cornerstone University, Grand Rapids, Michigan

"Gossip is a spark that starts countless relational fires every day. Matt provides practical, biblical guidance on how believers can reduce this insidious problem by bringing their tongues under the lordship of Christ."

—**Ken Sande**,
president of Relational Wisdom 360, Billings, Montana

"*You* have to read this book! I am just kidding. We *all* have to read this book. Isn't it amazing that most of us have never read a clear, pastoral and practical book on what Scripture says about gossip? Well, here it is. Matt will guide you through this topic in such a way that you will be convicted. I certainly was. But he will do more than that. He will give you ideas about how you can spread good news about others so that the church will be more united and God will be honored."

—**Edward T. Welch**,
counselor and faculty member at the
Christian Counseling & Educational Foundation (CCEF), Glenside, Pennsylvania;
author of *Shame Interrupted*, *When People Are Big and God Is Small*,
Depression: A Stubborn Darkness and *Running Scared: Fear, Worry, and the God of Rest*

"Matthew Mitchell's book on resisting gossip helped me greatly, and the timing of it was perfect. I want to thank him for his wise and godly counsel straight from our Father's heart. I can hear the author's voice, and it doesn't beat me up. It challenges and exhorts but shows me that we are in this together for much good."

—**Jani Ortlund**,
author of *Fearlessly Feminine* and *His Loving Law, Our Lasting Legacy*;
speaker with Renewal Ministries, Nashville, Tennessee

"This book is excellent. Sweet and winsome in its presentation. Humble, yet biblically reasoned, 'an apple of gold in settings of silver.' I pray that it will be used greatly in local churches. It is good stuff and MUCH needed."

—**Chris Brauns**,
author of *Unpacking Forgiveness* and *When the Word Leads Your Pastoral Search*;
pastor of The Congregational Christian Church, Stillman Valley, Iowa

IN PRAISE OF . . .

"In *Resisting Gossip* experienced pastor Matt Mitchell skillfully tackles one of the most overlooked and destructive sins within the church. Dr. Mitchell's wise, biblical approach carefully defines gossip (no one excluded here!) and gets to the heart of both the causes and cures of this problem. Full of scriptural insight, practical examples and thoughtful questions for group discussion, this one-of-a-kind book aims to do nothing less than transform the way we speak to and about one another. Whether you are a perpetrator of gossip or a victim of gossip (invariably both!), you will surely find tangible help and Christ-centered hope in its pages."

—**Michael R. Emlet**,
M.Div., M.D., counselor and faculty member at the
Christian Counseling & Educational Foundation (CCEF), Glenside, Pennsylvania;
author of *CrossTalk: Where Life and Scripture Meet*

"Jesus never gossiped. The One who loves me and gave Himself for me wants me to do battle in my heart, and one of the intense battlefronts is gossip. With this book Mitchell aims to help me win that war with gospel power. Along the way he strategizes about the "principle of overflow," how to "pray and weigh," and five types of gossip that show me that though I may not think I have a gossipy heart in one sense, I might in another sense. This book aims at helping the reader repay evil with good."

—**Sam Crabtree**,
executive pastor at Bethlehem Baptist Church, Minneapolis, Minnesota;
author of *Practicing Affirmation: God-Centered Praise of Those Who Are Not God*

"Does the gospel have anything to say about gossip? Matt Mitchell's engaging writing demonstrates that every Christian needs to understand the hope-giving promises of the gospel for addressing the heart issues behind gossip. Building upon a relevant biblical definition of gossip, *Resisting Gossip* empowers believers to apply the gospel to uproot the weeds of gossip. Mitchell's principles for cultivating a gossip-resistant church are worth the price of the book."

—**Bob Kellemen**,
Ph.D., executive director of the Biblical Counseling Coalition, Lafayette, Indiana;
author of *Equipping Counselors for Your Church*

"Matt Mitchell did not casually put this book together but asked lots of questions, explored lots of complicated situations and aimed for biblical wisdom that truly applies to all. The book is great for the home groups at my church to consider walking through together."

—**Diane McDougall**,
editorial director at Journey Group, Charlottesville, Virginia;
editor of EFCA Today

"Matt Mitchell tackles one of the most common, destructive but least talked about sins. While gossip destroys, Matt suggests alternatives to gossip that build trust and relationship and that are practical and helpful. Our words, good and bad, are powerful, and this book can be a helpful tool in prompting God's people to consider their words, attitudes and practices. I highly recommend it."

—**T.J. Addington**,
executive director of ReachGlobal, Minneapolis, Minnesota;
author of *Leading from the Sandbox, High-Impact Church Boards, Live Like You Mean It* and *When Life Comes Undone*

"This book provides a great balance between exposing and articulating the heart problem of gossip and revealing and articulating the gospel's answer to that problem. The book applies several well-known passages of Scripture to the topic of gossip that I had not previously seen applied in this manner. Many other lesser-known scriptures came alive to me by their application to gossip. I already am recommending this book—and quoting it."

—**Dan Ledford**,
pastor of Westminster Presbyterian Church in America, Butler, Pennsylvania

"Matthew Mitchell's book is personal and loving instead of simply academic and informational. I appreciated his open, honest self-disclosure. I really liked the simple definitions, especially of gossip and of judging. Matt makes it clear that our heart is the core issue in the problem of gossip as well as the place in which change happens through confession, repentance, grace and the work of the Spirit. This book will be extremely helpful in clarifying, diagnosing and healing the sin of gossip in individuals and in churches. It is simple, deep and easy reading all at the same time."

—**Bruce Weatherly**,
director of Safe Harbor Christian Counseling of Mid-Pennsylvania

"The foundational strength of *Resisting Gossip* isn't found in just a single chapter. It runs through the whole book. That strength is the good news, the gospel. Not the three-point outline that gets a person 'saved' but the impact of the gospel that redeems, justifies, propitiates and sanctifies. Too often authors who take on topical issues such as gossip tip their hat to the gospel, assume it as an underlying principle or ignore it altogether. Not so in this material. The gospel is front and center and applied throughout all the suggestive material in how to deal with resisting gossip."

—**Dennis W. Wadsworth, Jr.**,
pastor at Hope Evangelical Free Church, Fertile, Minnesota

"This book presents real-life examples that I can identify with. They are engaging because, let's be honest, we love to hear a good story. The reader is drawn in by the example and then confronted with the spiritual ramifications of gossip because of the book's biblical content and teaching on the subject of gossip. The supporting references and practical advice do not leave much room for misunderstanding. On the contrary, they bring one to the point at which the reader's final decision has to be a matter of the heart, before God and man."

—**Jaroslav Elijas**,
director at Christian Evangelistic Center, Serbia;
assistant pastor at Glozan Baptist Church, Serbia

"Dr. Mitchell not only walks alongside us as a brother in Christ to help us understand the subject of gossip, but he also gives a proactive, biblical and applicable plan of how to deal with it through the changing of our own hearts. This book is an excellent resource within our School of Discipleship."

—**Matt Cox**,
executive director of Miracle Mountain Ranch Missions Inc., Spring Creek, PA;
homeschool father of five

"This book on gossip meets a huge need. It is a response to a problem within the church as well as in individual lives. I would recommend it to all Christians and more specifically to pastors. There is precious little on this topic."

—**Tim McIntosh**,
author of *Leadership Peruvian Style*;
director of general studies at the Evangelical Seminary of Lima, Peru

"I thoroughly enjoyed and was challenged by Matt's biblical approach to gossip. As a district superintendent with the EFCA, I too often experience the fruit of gossip in churches. I believe that Matt's work has great opportunities for individuals as well as groups to learn to biblically deal with gossip. I especially like the questions at the end of each chapter and believe they make the material very applicable for small groups. I believe this subject must be addressed in the church today."

—**Jeff Powell**,
Allegheny district superintendent of the Evangelical Free Church of America (EFCA),
Minneapolis, Minnesota

"Gossip is such a pervasive and insidious problem that it's amazing there are so few resources to help churches deal with its destructive power. Matt's book is an incredibly useful tool that I expect to have wide impact in dealing with the problem of gossip. It is thoroughly biblical, loaded with wisdom and immensely practical. Just as importantly, it is written in an engaging and accessible style. I can't recommend it more highly."

—**Winston T. Smith**,
counselor and faculty member at the
Christian Counseling & Educational Foundation (CCEF), Glenside, Pennsylvania;
author of *Marriage Matters: Extraordinary Change Through Ordinary Moments*

Resisting Gossip

Published by CLC Publications

U.S.A.
P.O. Box 1449, Fort Washington, PA 19034

GREAT BRITAIN
51 The Dean, Alresford, Hants. SO24 9BJ

© 2013 by CLC Publications
All rights reserved. Published 2013

ISBN (*trade paper*): 978-1-61958-076-3
ISBN (*e-book*): 978-1-61958-077-0

Printed in the United States of America

19 18 17 16 15 14 13 12 11   1 2 3 4 5 6

Unless otherwise noted, Scripture quotations are from the Holy Bible, New International Version®, NIV®, © 1973, 1978, 1984, 2011 by Biblica. Used by permission of Zondervan. All rights reserved worldwide.

Scripture quotations marked NLT are from the Holy Bible, New Living Translation, © 1996, 2004, 2007 by Tyndale House Foundation. Used by permission of Tyndale House Publishers, Inc., Carol Stream, Illinois 60188. All rights reserved.

Scripture quotations marked KJV are from the Holy Bible, King James Version, 1611.

The Message, © 1993, 1994, 1995, 1996, 2000, 2001, 2002. Used by permission of NavPress Publishing Group.

Scripture quotations marked NASB are from the New American Standard Bible®, © 1960, 1962, 1963, 1968, 1971, 1972, 1973, 1975, 1977, 1995 by The Lockman Foundation. Used by permission.

Italics in Scripture quotations are the emphasis of the author.

To my Heather Joy:
Sweetheart, you don't need this book.
"She speaks with wisdom,
and faithful instruction is on her tongue."
Proverbs 31:26

In loving memory of Linda Jane Lundeen
February 28, 1951–December 10, 2010

Nana, we miss your stories.

Contents

Foreword by Edward T. Welch 11
Introduction 15

PART 1: Recognizing Gossip

1. What, Exactly, Is Gossip? 21
   A Biblical Definition of Sinful Gossip
2. Why Do We Gossip? 35
   The Heart of Gossip
3. A Gallery of Gossips 45
   Five Kinds of Gossiping People

PART 2: Resisting Gossip

4. Believing the Best 63
   Charitable Judgments Undo Gossip
5. Instead of Gossip: Speaking 77
   Putting off Gossip and Putting on Edifying Speech
6. Instead of Gossip: Listening 93
   What to Do When Gossip Comes Your Way

PART 3: Responding to Gossip

7. Responding in Faith 109
   Trusting God with My Reputation
8. Responding in Love...123
   Loving My Enemies?

PART 4: Regretting Gossip

9. Regretting Gossip..139
   Gossip Seems Irresistible—What Happens After I Give In?
   Epilogue - A Final Word: The End of Gossip 151
   No More Bad News

Bonus Chapter: For Church Leaders

Cultivating a Gossip-resistant Church 155
*Loose Lips Sink Fellowships,
but the Gospel Wins the War of the Wagging Tongue*

Notes...175
Going Deeper: *Recommended Reading for Resisting Gossip*.........181
Acknowledgments 188
About the Author 191

Foreword

I came to this book, not because I thought I had a huge problem with gossip—who does?—but because I love Matt. With that in mind, I'll first introduce Matt then get to the book itself.

The Person

I want Matt to be my pastor. I want to move to rural Pennsylvania, maybe move in with his family, learn from his preaching, and watch him love people wisely and well. You will want that, too. He is one of those rare people who can say the hardest thing to you and you will find it so helpful that you'll ask for more.

He knows how to say the right thing and he knows how to say it well. Check out his blog for more evidence. He is so clear in what he says and writes. So personal. So accessible. You will see that clarity right from the beginning when you read his definition of gossip: "sinful gossip is bearing bad news behind someone's back out of a bad heart." That is memorable and gets to the point. "Stinky words", far from being just a clever phrase, will also stick in your mind as he shows you how it is a reasonable translation of a biblical word used for gossip.

He loves his family. What a great dedication at the front of this book. It brings tears to my eyes and shows his tenderness.

He is the anti-gossip. You will read a number of stories in

what is ahead, and like nearly every person in them. Matt bears good news about congregants and friends.

He knows Scripture very well and it is part of him. Scripture is deep and sophisticated—yet is understandable to children; it says hard things, but it is truly good news and it should sound that way; it is fresh and lively; it should never seem canned, trite, hackneyed or boring. You will get all this from Matt. He embodies these attributes, and he writes this way, too.

Think of him as a friend. A friend is a very high calling. A friend is open with his or her own life, walks *with* us rather than far out in front, never talks down, has our best interests at heart, and, somehow, we let down our guard in a friend's presence. Think of him as a *trusted* friend.

The Book

Regarding the book, everyone should read at least one book about resisting gossip; every pastor should have this topic in the preaching rotation; and every small group should talk about it each year. Scripture identifies it as a pernicious problem (e.g., Prov. 26:22) and it deserves our careful attention.

The choices of reading material, surprisingly, are few. Perhaps we have assumed that gossip is one of those features of human nature that cannot change and so we celebrate it rather than fight against it. Matt suggests why this is: gossip is like "choice morsels." For me, that would mean M & M's. You might think you can resist them when they are out of sight, but they beckon and tantalize once in view. That insight alone makes the book worthwhile.

I can remember times when gossip was a choice morsel for me. I thought I had grown in these things. I don't speak gossip that often, but I can listen to it when it is available, and I am still attracted to the covers of the tabloids and *People* magazine.

So yes, be prepared for conviction. Better yet, look forward to it. Conviction is sweet when the one who brings it has our best interests in mind, and it is certainly sweet when our God is quick to forgive and speaks good words to us and about us.

The wonderfully practical steps in *Resisting Gossip* give clear direction to that conviction. They show us a way out of gossip that is wise, not formulaic, always fixing our minds on Jesus, and they replace gossip with a rich vision for how to be a bearer of good news about people who are commendable and even about those who are rascals.

People who are guilty of gossip are also hurt by it. How pastoral and protective of Matt to include a significant section of this book to gossip's destruction. It is so painful for the maligned. For them, Matt maps out a path that is hard, and can only be done in prayerful dependence on Jesus, but that path is so good. He got me excited to love people who acted as my enemies.

> If people have gossiped about you, make sure that your basic stance is *for them*. This doesn't mean that you must trust them in the same way you did before they gossiped about you. It does mean you should want what is best for them, even at a personal cost. That is how Jesus loved us, isn't it? While we were still His enemies, Christ died for us (see Rom. 5:8).

His last chapter gives recommendations for church leaders. They are in a complicated predicament when it comes to gossip. They know it can bring down a church, as well as their own ministry; every pastor has been victimized by gossip. But a pastor cannot easily say, "Stop gossiping about your leaders—that is, me— and honor me as Scripture says." Matt brings essential guidance on these matters.

If you are not a pastor, be sure to either give this book to yours when you are done or, buy an extra copy.

Thank you, Matt. You have pastored us well with your diligent labors.

Edward T. Welch
CCEF

Introduction

Gossip is everywhere.

Need proof? Check your Facebook. Flip on the television. Scan the magazine rack at the checkout counter. Listen closely to the conversations around you at work, at school, or in the neighborhood. How often do you hear or say, "I shouldn't tell you this, but . . ." or, "It's none of my business, but . . ." or, "Have you heard the latest about . . . ?" Ears perk up. Eyebrows rise. Bodies lean in. Voices lower. We're hooked.

Gossip is something that we all experience. No one is safe from its tantalizing lure. No one is safe from its poisonous effects.

And yet, there is a surprising and sad lack of teaching on the subject for Christians. When was the last time you heard a sermon on the sin of gossip? The Bible is bursting with wisdom on the subject, and yet this teaching has hardly been noticed. This book is an attempt to arm followers of Christ with the biblical weapons we need to resist gossip in all its forms.

The Allure of Gossip

Gossip *is* hard to resist.

Why? For one, it is hard to define. There is a lot of confusion about what gossip is (and is not). When is it okay to talk about others, and when is it wrong? In chapter 1 I offer a biblically based definition: *the sin of gossip is bearing bad news behind someone's back out of a bad heart.* I explain this definition in great detail and show you where I get it from the Bible.

Chapter 2 explains why we gossip. The key to true change is understanding the last phrase in my definition, "out of a bad heart." We gossip because our sinful hearts are attracted to bad stories like moths to a flame.

Let me share with you a bit of my personal struggle with gossip. I'm an information junkie. I want to be in the know and to have a finger on the pulse of what's happening now. Can you relate? Of course, technology just feeds my addiction. With blog posts, status updates and e-mails, I crave the feeling of control that information gives me.

But that sense of control is just an illusion. I don't control anything. Instead, my addiction to information often controls me. But there's good news! Jesus Christ is changing my heart, and there are great and precious promises in His Word that the Lord is using to wean me off my information addiction and onto a love for and trust in Him.

A thirst for information may not be your personal temptation. In chapter 3 of this book, I sketch out five different kinds of gossiping people who are motivated by five different heart desires. If you do not find yourself somewhere among them, I'll be surprised.

Even when we know what gossip is and where it comes from, it is still hard to resist. It is hard to see any alternatives. What do you do *instead* of gossiping? Chapters 4, 5 and 6 provide biblical strategies for holding out against gossip and replacing it with loving thoughts, words and actions.

The Pain of Gossip

It is likely you initially picked up this book not because you have been tempted by gossip but because you've been hurt by it.

People have been gossiping about *you*, and it aches like a knife wound (see Prov. 12:18). Your reputation has been dragged through the mud, and you're not sure anymore who your true friends are. Chapters 7 and 8 are written for you. They explain what the Bible says we are supposed to do when we have become the target of sinful gossip.

I've been there too. As a pastor, there have been times when I've been the subject of gossip in our little community. In fact, I'll share with you a few stories in later chapters (although names and identifying characteristics have been changed to protect reputations—I do not want to gossip in a book about resisting gossip!). One time, when the gossip was at its worst, I thought seriously about quitting the pastorate altogether. But I'm glad I didn't. God has been faithful to me, and He will be to you, as well.

The Wickedness of Gossip

Sometimes gossip does not seem like such a big deal. The English word "gossip" only appears a handful of times in the whole Bible. But every time it shows up, it spells trouble. The apostle Paul denounces those who gossip alongside murderers and God-haters in a list of "every kind of wickedness, evil, greed, and depravity" (Rom. 1:29), saying that those who do these things deserve death (see 1:28–32). The apostle James says that although our tongues are small, they are capable of great evil. He says that gossiping is playing with fire (see James 3:2–6). Though gossip is everywhere and so alluring, it must be resisted—not just because it hurts people but because it offends a holy God.

Unfortunately, we have all been guilty of offending God by gossiping at some point, and we can't just take our words back. Where do we go when we've already given in? In chapter 9, we learn what the Bible says about true repentance and the hope we have in the grace of God through Jesus Christ.

*   *   *

If you are a pastor or church leader who wants to strengthen your local fellowship against the dangers of gossip, you might want to have study groups read this book together. Group discussion questions at the end of each chapter focus on applying key scriptures. There is also a bonus chapter at the end of the book containing biblical principles for your leadership team to consider as you cultivate a gossip-resistant church.

I'm thankful for my church family, Lanse Evangelical Free Church, for making it so easy for me to write this book. When one guy heard that I was writing on gossip, he asked me, "Oh, do you have *that* problem in your church?" I was able to truthfully say, "No. We don't have a gossipy church." That makes it much easier for me to teach on this subject. We're not perfect, but we are committed to spiritual unity and have learned a few things along the way.

The Resistibility of Gossip through Christ

There *is* hope. You and I are not left on our own to deal with the allure, pain and wickedness of gossip. God's "divine power has given us everything we need for life and godliness through our knowledge of him who called us by his own glory and goodness" (2 Pet. 1:3). The gospel of Jesus Christ defeats gossip. Turn the page, and we'll begin to see how.

PART 1

RECOGNIZING GOSSIP

*The words of a gossip are like choice morsels;
they go down to a man's inmost parts.*

Proverbs 18:8, 26:22

1

What, Exactly, Is Gossip?

The first rule of war is to know your enemy.

Before we can resist gossip, we must recognize it. That's not as easy to do as it may sound. It is not always easy to recognize the moment when our "small talk" becomes sinful talk. In fact, if you're like me, then you regularly ask yourself during conversations, "Should I be saying this?" or, "Should I be listening to this?"

You may even find yourself questioning what makes gossip wrong. Is it *when* it is said? *Who* says it? To *whom* it is told? We often give ourselves small passes. Gossip is okay if we're just chatting with our wife or sister, right? Or if we're just "venting" to our mom or pastor, right? What is gossip, anyway? Is it always a lie? Is it always an unsubstantiated rumor? Is gossip always malicious? The line becomes increasingly fuzzy as confusion sets in about the definition of gossip. Deciding what is or isn't gossip is certainly a challenge.

The hardest part about recognizing gossip is that it does not come with a warning label. Wouldn't it be great if a sign like this would flash above the heads of the people with whom we're talking?

> **WARNING!**
> **The contents of the next conversation contain sinful gossip. Use extreme caution.**

Then again, I'm not sure I would like that. Too often it might show up over *my* head!

Nevertheless, this is not what happens, is it? No, normally, there we are, just talking with someone, and seemingly out of nowhere this juicy piece of news about someone else presents itself and asks us to swallow it. The Bible says, "The words of a gossip are like choice morsels; they go down to a man's inmost parts" (Prov. 18:8, 26:22). This proverb is so important that the Lord made sure it was in the book of Proverbs twice! Let me explain what it means.

Choice Morsels

"Choice morsels" are tasty things that we want to devour quickly. They are the best, most attractive, most addictive things to eat. They are like a bowl of potato chips left on the kitchen counter.

What happens in most families if Mom puts a bowl of Doritos (or substitute your favorite salty snack here) out on the kitchen counter in the late afternoon? I don't know about your family, but at our place, those things are gone like the wind! My wife, Heather Joy, has gotten wise to this and now puts out a bowl of apples or carrots. And *they* are gone long before supper.

But let's say there are Doritos on the counter. What happens if you eat the whole bag before supper yourself? Unless you have the constitution of an ox, you're probably going to feel sick. Gossip is like that. It goes "down to a man's inmost parts." My grandma had a magnet on her fridge with a picture of a pig that said, "Once across the lips, always on the hips." Gossip tastes great going down, but it has lasting and poisonous effects on our hearts.

But again, what *is* sinful gossip?

I'm glad you asked.

Here is a one-sentence summary of the Bible's teaching on gossip: *Sinful gossip is bearing bad news behind someone's back out of a bad heart.* This definition has three main parts.

Definition Part 1: Bearing Bad News

Gossip is, obviously, a "talking" thing. As we saw, our opening scripture says, "The *words* of a gossip are like choice morsels." Gossip is sharing, communicating and transmitting stories. These stories flow in both directions: talking and listening.

First, *talking*. Proverbs says, "A gossip betrays a confidence; so avoid a man who *talks* too much" (20:19). The old King James word for a gossip in Proverbs 20:19 is a "talebearer," or one who carries a story. Gossiping is often sharing someone else's secret. Have you ever done that? I must admit that I have, to my shame. Have you ever had it done *to* you? It feels awful to find out that someone gave away your secret. It is a betrayal by talking.

Then there is *listening*. Proverbs also says, "Wrongdoers eagerly *listen* to gossip; liars pay close attention to slander" (17:4, NLT). Sometimes even just receiving that spicy piece of gossip without stopping the conversation (or, at least, saying *something*) is sinful—almost as sinful as speaking it.

Online Gossip

Of course, this bearing of bad news is not done by just talking in person. Technology has made it possible for us to gossip long distance. We can gossip on the phone. We can gossip online. We can tweet our gossip on Twitter!

I love the Internet. As of this writing, I subscribe to 357 blogs in my blog reader and have hundreds of friends on Facebook. It is a great way to stay in touch with people. But anything that can be used for great good can also be used for great evil, especially if it involves a lot of words. The Bible teaches this: "When words are many, sin is not absent, but he who holds his tongue is wise" (Prov. 10:19).

So sinful gossip for me might be pressing the "Send" button on my phone, the "Publish" button on my blog or the "Share" button on my Facebook account. Remember, whatever is said online is pretty much permanent. Think first!

A few years ago a friend of mine sent a negative e-mail about a mutual acquaintance of ours not to me but, by mistake, to the person herself! Oops. Did *that* ever cause bad feelings! You and I may never press the wrong "Send To" button, but what kinds of stories have we been sharing about others via technology?

Three Types of Bad News

The content of sinful gossip is never neutral. It is always "bad news" of at least one of three kinds.

Bad information. Sharing bad information—lies—about someone behind their back is sinful gossip. Worse, if you *know* that a story is false, then it is not just gossip, it is also slander! Have you ever had your reputation hurt by bad information that someone had spread about you?

I have. Once I heard through the grapevine of our little community a circulating rumor that said I had left my wife. This was laughable to anyone who really knows us (I don't know how I could live without her!). I have no idea who started the rumor or who might have heard it and believed the lie.

The Lord promises us that "a false witness will not go unpunished, and he who pours out lies will not go free" (Prov. 19:5).

Of course, the "bad" information might be something that you *think* is true but really is not. You *think* that your neighbor got a DUI, but you got the story wrong. Or it might be something unverifiable such as rumor or hearsay, as in my case. Either way, it's gossip.

Bad news about *someone*. On the other hand, the story being shared might actually be true and only *about* something bad that someone has done. This is what I call a shameful truth. Some of us have been taught that if something is true, then it's not gossip. Not so. Gossip is also foolishly spreading that awful truth about someone. Proverbs tells us that "a gossip betrays a confidence, but a trustworthy man keeps a secret" (11:13). The secrets revealed by gossip are often the skeletons in someone's closet that do not really need to get out.

A biblical phrase for this is "a bad report" (Hebrew *dibbah*). A bad report is what Joseph brought to Jacob about his brothers in Genesis 37:2. We don't know exactly what the young men were up to, but given what we do know about Joseph's ten brothers, it was probably something they shouldn't have been doing. So Joseph was probably not lying, but he was, at the very least, being an annoying tattletale. Tattling is gossiping to someone in authority instead of someone uninvolved. Proverbs says, "Whoever spreads slander [*dibbah*] is a fool" (10:18).

For example, let's say one of your friends recently did something bad, and you heard about it. Maybe it was even your friend who told you about it. He cut someone off in traffic. She lied to her spouse. He cheated a coworker. She hit her mother. Whatever. Your friend actually did some shameful thing.

Catch this: *you don't have to talk about any of it with your other friends!*

I know it's hard to refrain. As our key Scripture passage says, "The words of a gossip are like choice morsels." They are incredibly difficult to resist.

By the way, you may have memorized Proverbs 18:8 and 26:22 in the King James Version, and right now you may be scratching your head and saying, "Hey, wait a minute! That verse says, 'The words of a talebearer are *as wounds*'! There's a big difference between wounds and choice morsels!"

The reason for the difference between the two versions is that the translators of the King James Bible thought that the Hebrew root word being used here was one that means to hammer or strike something (*halam*). And that rings true, doesn't it? The words of a gossip are harmful. They are a kick in the gut.

But most scholars today believe that there is a different Hebrew root underlying this word: *laham*. This root word depicts savory or delicious morsels that you can hardly resist and want to swallow right down.[1]

My wife, Heather Joy, makes candies called Buckeyes. They are like homemade Reese's Peanut Butter Cups, but better. The candy is chocolate on the outside with sweet peanut butter on the inside. My wife almost has to lock the cabinet, however, after making them, because I can't say no to them. If she offers me a Buckeye, I don't care how many platefuls I have just eaten or how full I am. I'll find the room! Those candies are "choice morsels."

Back in Solomon's day a choice morsel wasn't made of chocolate and peanut butter. It may have been various nuts and raisins or figs mixed with honey for something sweet to eat. Or, even more likely, it was a choice piece of meat. Whenever roast beef is being cooked, my oldest son, Andrew, always says, "Can I have a piece with some fat on it?" *That* is an example of a choice morsel! It is difficult to resist.

Bad news, shameful news, is like that too for you and me. Bad news is attractive but not good for us. There is something really wrong within us that makes us want to know and to talk about the shameful things that other people do.

Bad news for *someone*. A third kind of bad news is neither false nor true but is a projection of something bad happening to someone. In Psalm 41 King David got really sick, and his enemies rejoiced and started to gossip about him. David wrote,

> My enemies say of me in malice, "When will he die and his name perish?" Whenever one comes to see me, he speaks falsely, while his heart gathers slander; then he goes out and spreads it abroad. All my enemies whisper together against me; they imagine the worst for me, saying, "A vile disease has beset him; he will never get up from the place where he lies." (41:5–8)

That is gossip too. David had not done anything shameful, but his enemies were two-faced. They came in saying, "Oh, poor you," and then went out to spread the bad news that he was going to die.

Have you ever had this happen to you? People say, "He's going to lose his job" or, "He's not going to make the team." They project, "She's going to get kicked out of school" or, "Her husband is going to leave her." They whisper, "They're going to lose their house." Gossip is bad news wickedly projected for someone else.

Definition Part 2: Behind Someone's Back

By anyone's definition gossip happens when the person you are talking about *is not there*. Some translations of Proverbs 18:8

and 26:22 use the word "whisperer" instead of "gossip" or "talebearer." A whisperer is someone who talks about you behind your back. Therefore, gossip is clandestine—and intentionally so!

You see, it is so much easier (and more interesting) to talk about someone when they are not around. Before you talk (or before you continue to talk) about someone who is not present, ask yourself the following:

- Would I say this if he were here? (Really? Be honest now.)
- Would I receive this bad news about her in the same way if she were present?
- Am I hiding this conversation from someone?
- Would I want someone else to talk this way about me if I were out of the room?

Yeah, But What About . . . ?

Let me clear up a possible misunderstanding. The Bible is not teaching that we should never talk about people who are not present. We certainly can say good things about people who are not with us. In fact, we absolutely should turn gossip around and spread good news about people!

Also, there are times when we have to talk about people who are not present and even share bad things about them. Parents, teachers, elders and pastors, even friends, teammates, coworkers and neighbors all have to do that sometimes. This falls in line with the biblical principle of *warning others*, which we'll learn more about in chapter 5.

I once heard of a Christian couple who tried really hard to resist gossip. This man and his wife would not say anything about someone who was not in the same room as they were. Nothing.

Not even a positive word! How long do you think that worked?

Sometimes we need to seek counsel from a wise person about our conflicts and problems. Seeking counsel may involve sharing the shameful things that someone else has done without that person being there. It is certainly not sinful gossip to truly seek out help. On the other hand, we can often mask our desire to gossip by claiming that we are just seeking counsel. The key to sharing circumstances with people in a right way is to keep loving others even when we have to talk about them and even if they are our enemies. We'll dig into this more in chapter 8, but simply put, we just need to apply Jesus' Golden Rule to any difficult situation. If you have to talk about someone when they are not present, make sure that you are treating them as you would want to be treated.

Definition Part 3: Out of a Bad Heart

Gossip comes out of a bad heart. That is, gossip is caused by something that is wrong at the core of our beings. *We are attracted to the "choice morsels" of gossip because of something already wrong in our "inmost parts."* Accepting this is the most important key to resisting gossip.

The Lord Jesus taught that "out of the overflow of the heart the mouth speaks" (Matt. 12:34). The heart is the control center of a person. It is the inner you, the real you. The Bible also teaches that we live from our hearts. Proverbs says, "Above all else, guard your heart, for it is the wellspring of life" (4:23). Our motives spring from our hearts. Our sinful motivations for speaking about or listening to any form of bad news are what makes gossip sinful. Therefore, in recognizing gossip the most important question for us to answer is, "Why?"

- Why am I saying this?

- Why am I listening to this?
- Why am I attracted to this bad news?

It could be because of jealousy or anger or hate. Or it could be the result of boredom, pride, or the fear of people. There are a number of sinful heart motivations that can produce sinful gossip. The good news is that the gospel of Jesus Christ has answers for them all.

Resistance Is *Not* Futile

Proverbs 18:8 and 26:22 offer only a warning: "Beware of gossip." They do not tell us how to resist those choice morsels—just that we need to. But now that we have a biblically informed definition to use when we attempt to recognize gossip, we can begin to think more clearly about gospel strategies for resisting gossip. Some of those strategies include:

- Bearing good news
- Being up front, and loving those we talk about and talk to
- Having a changed heart that loves God and loves people

When I was a teen, I was a big fan of *Star Trek: The Next Generation*. The greatest enemy of the crew of the Starship *Enterprise* during that particular incarnation of the Star Trek series was a species called the Borg. A race of aliens, the Borg were basically part of one great, big machine that swallowed up whole cultures into its system. There was no individualism in the Borg, just "the collective." When the Borg came to town, their favorite phrase was, "Resistance is futile! You will be assimilated."

I know that's how gossip often makes us feel—that we must

conform to the world's gossipy pattern. *It is not true.* Jesus Christ died to set us free from sin. "He himself bore our sins in his body on the tree, so that we might die to sins and live for righteousness" (1 Pet. 2:24). Resistance is not futile. Doesn't the Bible insist that we are to "resist the devil, and he will flee" (James 4:7)? The Lord Jesus empowers us to die to sins and to live for righteousness. One of the chief ways He does that is through promises like the one we find in First Corinthians 10:13.

A Great and Precious Promise: A Way Out

The apostle Paul told the Corinthians (and, through them, us too), "No temptation has seized you except what is common to man" (1 Cor. 10:13). The urge to gossip is not extraordinary. We should not feel as if we are the first to ever experience it. I'm sure that even the Lord Jesus was tempted to gossip (although, praise God, He never gave in; see Heb 4:15).

But Paul went on to say, "And God is faithful; he will not let you be tempted beyond what you can bear" (1 Cor. 10:13). We have to believe what Paul said, even though it will seldom feel as if it is true.

Paul finished the verse with the promise, "But when you are tempted, [God] will also provide a way out so that you can stand up under it" (10:13). What a great and precious promise! Our job is to trust God's promise and to look for the "way out" which will always be available. The temptation may not go away. We may even have to continue to "stand up under it." Yet although it is not easy, it is possible to win against sinful gossip.

Questions for Group Discussion

1. What are some popular conceptions and misconceptions of gossip? Before you read this chapter, how would you have defined gossip?

2. Discuss the book's definition of sinful gossip: bearing bad news behind someone's back out of a bad heart. In what ways does this definition expand or sharpen your concept of gossip? How is it helpful (or unhelpful) for recognizing sinful gossip in everyday life? Give an example.

3. Read Proverbs 18:8 or 26:22. In what ways is gossip like a "choice morsel"? Why is gossip so attractive and addictive? How does it affect us?

4. Read First Peter 2:13–25. How does Jesus' death enable Christians to live for righteousness? How does the gospel defeat gossip?

5. Read First Corinthians 10:13. How can you apply this great and precious promise to gossip this week?

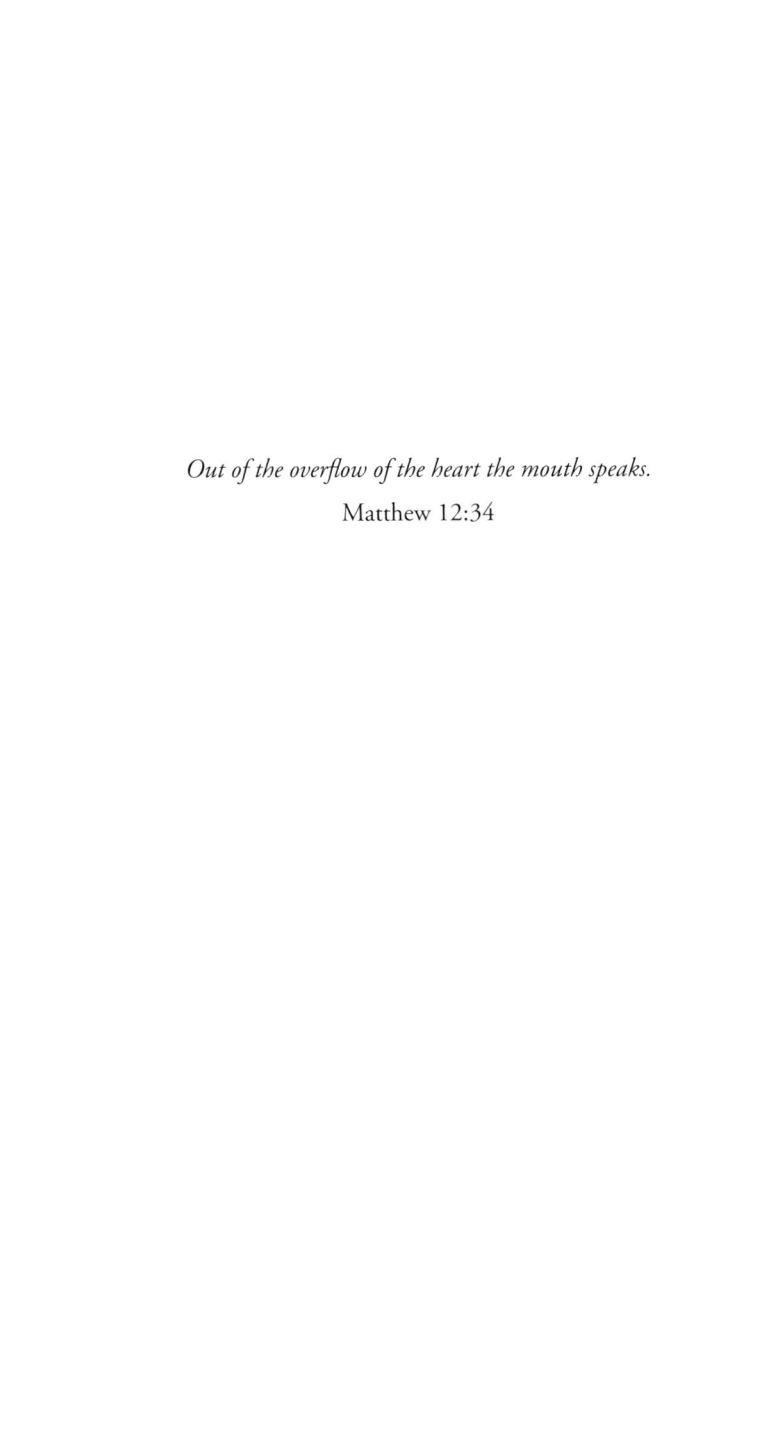

Out of the overflow of the heart the mouth speaks.
Matthew 12:34

2

Why Do We Gossip?

Everyone loves a story.

From the time our children were first born, my wife and I read stories to them. We would prop the babies up in my wife's lap and open colorful little board books about "great green" rooms, a curious monkey called George, a little engine that could, a sourpuss donkey named Eeyore and many more. These books didn't just introduce numbers, colors and letters. They told stories that helped our kids understand their world.

The kids are bigger now, but they still love stories. My daughter, Robin, doesn't read books—she devours them. One year she read 382 books, more than a book per day. The vast majority of those books were full of more than just useful information. Robin also read novels and biographies, all full of stories.

Even if some people do not like to read, everyone loves a story. We delight in hearing someone share a tale, whether it is funny, sad, strange or happy. And many of us love to tell stories ourselves.

At church we have a couple of storytellers who have a yarn for every occasion—stories that will either teach you something or will leave you in stitches. Some will do both! The guys at the local restaurant seem to be able to sit for hours and do little more than shoot the breeze, telling story after story. Even as I've been writing this chapter, I've clicked over to my Facebook newsfeed to catch up on what's happening with my friends. Some of them can tell quite a story in just a paragraph!

My mother-in-law Linda loved stories. In fact, she *thought* in stories. If someone had pricked her, she would have bled narrative. "Nana" went to be with the Lord in December of 2010, and we miss her storytelling. For us she was the glue that held our extended family together over a vast distance. Heather Joy was on the phone with her every week sharing all the funny little things the grandchildren had done and listening as Linda shared news about our extended family sprinkled across the continent. Now that Nana is gone, we've had a much harder time staying in touch with family members. No stories from Nana to connect us all.

The Old, Old Story

Stories are an integral part of our lives. They are how we figure out our world and our place in it. The Bible is full of stories. Most of the Old Testament and all of the Gospels and Acts are narratives. The other parts of Scripture, such as the Psalms, the Proverbs and the Letters, include loads of storytelling features. All these biblical stories are like tributaries that are carried along and then joined together to form one great river—the grand story of redemption.

One summary of this great story says, "For God so loved the world that he gave his one and only Son, that whoever believes in him shall not perish but have eternal life" (John 3:16). Eternal life and eternal death are bound up in our believing or not believing in the story of Jesus. The shorthand for this story is "the gospel." The gospel is news—the best story—and it is powerful. As the apostle Paul says, "I am not ashamed of the gospel, because it is the power of God for the salvation of everyone who believes" (Rom. 1:16).

So it is no wonder that we love stories! *We are living in one.*

Stories Gone Bad

The problem is not that we love stories but that we can love stories too much, and, especially, we can love the wrong stories. We saw in the last chapter that sinful gossip tells a bad story. It is bad news. And while there are times when sharing bad news is necessary (especially when it leads up to good news), bearing bad news can be antithetical to the gospel itself.

In Genesis 3 we read that the serpent in the garden told the woman a bad story about God. He questioned her, "Did God really say . . . ?" (3:1). The serpent slandered God's reputation, and when his bad story was believed, the effect was devastating on all human history. Every small bit of sinful gossip in daily life is an evil echo of what went wrong at the very beginning. In fact, gossip is the same ugly sin played out again and again. Gossip is believing the ancient lie that we can attempt to play God by destroying others with the power of our words. Gossip is not just breaking a rule; it is perversely living out Satan's lies, which we would rather believe than the truth.[1]

And therefore, sadly, we are attracted to the wrong stories. Bad news travels fast because it is popular. A few years ago a prominent Christian working in government was found to have been involved in petty theft. I don't know why, but I became addicted to his story. I kept searching the Internet for more details and reading every discussion about the situation that I could find on any blog. There was no good reason for me to inform myself about it, but I almost could not stop myself from digging for more. This is a perfect example of how our hearts are spring-loaded to love bad stories.

Gossip in the Teachers' Lounge

"Lynette" took a new job as a schoolteacher.[2] She liked the students and most of her coworkers, but she had a problem with gossip. Her problem was that *she liked it*.

> For several months, I kept my mouth shut and simply listened to the talk about campus. When asked a direct question about another teacher or our supervisor, whom my colleagues did not like, I would shrug and offer up that I had no opinion. Mind you, I did not *stop* any gossip. Instead, I was quite intrigued to find out what the "scoop" was around town. This was just the beginning for me . . . listening to the gossip without protesting.[3]

Lynette was attracted to the wrong kind of stories. She became addicted to listening to the "choice morsels" (Prov. 26:22) of gossip. Of course, it did not stop there. Her next step was to share some herself:

> It wasn't long before I had my own negative encounter with our supervisor. By this point, I had made several friends in the department and felt comfortable going to them with my issues. I wish I could say that I strictly presented the facts in a non-emotional way, but I never did. As a result, gossip started. Once this little tiny bit of juice spilled from my lips, it kept flowing, day after day, month after month, until I couldn't stop doing it. Even after the Holy Spirit convicted me that what I was doing was wrong, I still couldn't stop. My gossip finally caught up to me and got me in trouble with the person I had been speaking out against all this time. Even

after a confrontation, it was difficult to stop. The confrontation itself became a juicy piece of gossip to share with others.[4]

What went wrong with Lynette? From where did all that propensity to gossip come? The Lord Jesus says that it came out of her heart.

Overflow

In Matthew 12 we read that Jesus denounced the Pharisees for accusing Him of being in league with Satan. Their accusations were *bad words*, if I've ever heard any! Our Lord Jesus said,

> Make a tree good and its fruit will be good, or make a tree bad and its fruit will be bad, for a tree is recognized by its fruit. You brood of vipers, how can you who are evil say anything good? For *out of the overflow of the heart the mouth speaks*. The good man brings good things out of the good stored up in him, and the evil man brings evil things out of the evil stored up in him. But I tell you that men will have to give account on the day of judgment for every careless word they have spoken. For by your words you will be acquitted, and by your words you will be condemned. (12:33–37)

Let's call this *the principle of overflow*. We gossip (or say anything bad) because bad words overflow from our bad hearts.

Jesus likens people to trees. If the heart of the tree—the root system and trunk—is healthy, then the fruit of the tree will be good too. But if the root system is diseased, then the fruit will be worthless. We can tell what is in someone's heart by what comes out in the fruit. The same is true with us. Our words reveal what is in our hearts.

When I taught about this at our local church, I held up a bottle of water and then poured the water out on the platform.

Then I asked our church family, "Why is there now water on the floor?"[5]

Everybody giggled. I guess it was obvious.

Then I asked, "Why is there water on the floor and not Pepsi or Kool-Aid?"

Now besides the fact that I would have gotten into major trouble with the custodian if I had poured Pepsi or Kool-Aid on the carpet, the truth is, there was *water* on the floor because there had been *water* in the bottle. Similarly, Jesus said, "Out of the overflow of the heart the mouth speaks." What's inside us determines what comes out of us.

The Lord Jesus was saying that the Pharisees, being snakelike (living out the bad story from the Garden of Eden), *could* not say anything good. It was not in their nature. It was not in their heart. As Jesus said to them, "The good man brings good things out of the good stored up in him, and the evil man brings evil things out of the evil stored up in him" (Matt. 12:35).

Joseph Stowell, president of Moody Bible Institute when I was a student there, used to tell us, "All talk is heart talk." I didn't quite get that at the time. I thought Dr. Stowell was teaching that we always mean exactly what we say. But then, I wondered, what about lying, flattery, bearing false witness? I understand now that Dr. Stowell was teaching that everything that comes out of our mouths reflects something that is deep within.

That's what Jesus was saying. Good small talk, good stories, come from good that is "stored up" in the heart. Sinful gossip comes out of the evil that is "stored up" in the human heart.

This is true even for believers in Jesus who now have new hearts from God (see Ezek. 36:26). The residue of indwelling sin lingers within us and continues to create evil motivations even when we are Christ followers.

Back to Lynette

Sometimes we cannot correctly discern our own motives. I am sure that Lynette could easily have justified her behavior in the teachers' lounge. Our hearts can be very deceptive, even with ourselves. But God knows. The Bible teaches, "All a man's ways seem innocent to him, but motives are weighed by the Lord" (Prov. 16:2). It also says that "Death and Destruction lie open before the Lord—how much more the hearts of men!" (Prov. 15:11). God knows and understands what is going on inside of us, even when we do not.

Matthew 12 is not the only place in which we see Jesus teaching the principle of overflow. We read in Matthew 15 that Jesus also says, "Out of the heart come evil thoughts, murder, adultery, sexual immorality, theft, false testimony, slander" (15:19). It is not just our sinful words that proceed from the heart but all our sins—including *listening* to sinful gossip.

Lynette had a heart problem. She had allowed her heart to be hijacked by discontentment, self-righteous judgment and a lust for entertainment; and sinful gossip was the overflow. She believed Satan's bad story that instead of mirroring God by using her words to love Him supremely and to love her neighbor as she loved herself, she could take God's place and use people for her own pleasure.

This is very serious, because Jesus says that we will face a reckoning. In the Matthew 12 passage, He said, "I tell you that men will have to give account on the day of judgment for every *careless word* they have spoken. For by your words you will be acquitted, and by your words you will be condemned" (12:36–37).

That is sobering. Just think about giving an account, not just for every malicious word that you and I have spoken, but for every careless, aimless, idle word! Words are serious. They do not just hit the air and then drift away. They are remembered. God is listening, and we will have to answer to Him.

Change Is Possible

Lynette's story, however, has a good ending. Don't you just love a good ending to a story? Lynette broke free from her addiction to gossip. "I am happy to report that I have been able to stay 'sober' from gossip ever since. It's been over two years since I last succumbed in any amount of severity. But I know that I need to be careful so I am not lured into it again," she says.[6]

God is in the business of *changing* our hearts. Christians do still have indwelling sin, but our sin is not greater than our Savior! Our indwelling sin is much like Saddam Hussein hiding away in a spider hole, thinking that he can still regain power by trying to coordinate the wreaking of havoc on the new regime. Though still dangerous, sin is a defeated enemy. I like to say, "Sin is still resident, but it is not president!" The Bible says that we have been "set free from sin and have become slaves to God" (Rom. 6:22). The Lord is our new master, and He is really good.

Looking Ahead

So where do we go from here? How do we break away from the influence of sinful gossip?

The Bible tells us, "Do not conform any longer to the pattern of this world, but be transformed by the renewing of your mind" (Rom. 12:2). Our minds are renewed by turning away from sin in our hearts and trusting in God's "very great and precious promises, so that through them [we] may participate in the divine nature and escape the corruption in the world caused by evil desires" (2 Pet. 1:4). The Holy Spirit uses these promises to purify our hearts and to transform our lives.

Let's discover together, in the next few chapters, what some of those purifying promises are.

Questions for Group Discussion

1. Why does everyone love a story? What kinds of stories do you like?
2. What is the story in which we are living? How might you summarize the gospel story in only one minute? What effect does this big story have on all the little stories that make up our lives?
3. Read Matthew 12:33–37. Discuss the principle of overflow. What is "the heart" (12:34), and what is its connection to our words and actions? How is "all talk heart talk?" How does it make you feel to think about giving an account for "every careless word" (12:36) you speak?
4. Talk about Lynette's story. Where did Lynette go wrong? Can you identify with her? How do you imagine that she got out of her situation?
5. Discuss the idea that "sin is still resident, but it is not president!" by reading Romans 6:18–22 and 12:2. How is sin still a problem for a Christian, and how is it also a defeated enemy? How can that perspective change your relationship to sinful gossip right now?

They are gossips.
Romans 1:29

3

A Gallery of Gossips

The book of Proverbs is like a song from *Sesame Street*.

If you were a kid or a parent during the last forty-five years, you probably remember the song "The People in Your Neighborhood" from the popular kids show. This childhood ditty was a little different each time it was sung because it always introduced a new neighbor: a policeman, a fireman, a meter reader, a baker or a postman. The refrain went something like this: "Well, they're the people that you meet when you're walking down the street. They're the people that you meet each day."[1]

The point of the song was to help kids recognize the various kinds of people who live in their community and to know how to relate to them. It made children feel safe to know what was going on in their little world by helping them to understand the different kinds of people who populated it and how those people would generally act.

Proverbs does the same thing. The book categorizes people into somewhat exaggerated personalities so that disciples of the Lord can recognize these people when they run into them *or when they themselves are acting like them.* In the Proverbs it is not the policeman and the postman; it is the sluggard, the wayward wife, the hot-tempered man, the fool and at least two kinds of gossips.

In fact, throughout the Bible, nearly every time the word "gossip" appears, it is not the verb form of the word that shows up, as in a kind of speech, but the noun form, as in a kind of person—a gossip. The Bible is actually more interested in the people who are doing the speaking than it is in their words. Words are important, but they are simply the fruit, the overflow, of the heart.

A Gallery of Gossips

Gossips come in different shapes and sizes. They (we) are motivated by different things at different times. Just as the *Sesame Street* song characterizes certain people, I'd like to consider five different kinds of gossiping people that we might meet (or *be*) in everyday life. These five are certainly not the only types of gossips that exist in this world. Our hearts are very creative in mixing up new motivations! These are just five common types driven by at least five ordinary (but ungodly) motivations. As we consider each one, we need to remember to look deeper than the behavior, into the heart of the gossip. We should ask ourselves the following:

1. What does this gossiper want and believe?
2. What is ruling the person's heart? Who or what is he or she worshiping?
3. What kind of "poisonous liquid" is in the person's "heart bottle" that is overflowing in sinful gossip?

The Bible has a remedy, an antidote, for each type of gossip. There are very great and precious promises that speak specifically to each of these hijacked hearts and, when believed, renew our minds, de-conform us from the world and transform our words and lives.

Gossip 1: The Spy

"Meagan" grew up in a family in which nothing that anyone said was secret or sacred. Her family was full of "spies." She says,

> You could count on everything being passed on to aunts and grandmas, because that is just how it was. It was unnerving to have things spread all through the family. I learned to keep most things private, then I got the cold shoulder because I was "shutting people out." Meaning, I didn't tell them all the little details of my life as much anymore. I learned to put my guard up and preface most personal conversations with, "This is private—for you only." Well, sometimes even that wasn't enough! Some people actually thought that "for you only" included three aunts and their mother whom they normally talked to![2]

Proverbs says, "A gossip betrays a confidence, but a trustworthy man keeps a secret" (11:13). The Hebrew word translated as "gossip" is *rakil*, which means "a peddler (of secrets), a huckster/hawker, a deceiver, or a spy."[3] The English Standard Version uses the phrase "whoever goes about slandering" to translate *rakil*. We might use the word "informer."

Do you have someone like this in your life? Are *you* an informer? One of my friends calls this "the eager-eared, probing side of gossip. Sometimes, it's so stealthy I don't catch it right away. Some folks are so good at [probing that] they [simply] mention a word or two and then just analyze my expression or the stuttering."[4] Spies know how to wheedle a story out of us.

The spy is somebody who loves to get the dirt on someone and then use that information to his or her personal advantage. At first spies may seem trustworthy, but they really are not. As we saw, Scripture says, "A gossip [*rakil*] betrays a confidence, but a trustworthy man keeps a secret."

Don't talk to a spy, or *your* secrets may be the next ones to be spilled. So what is the motivation of a spy?

Power

Spies are primarily motivated by a hunger for *power*. There is something that a spy wants, and such a person will use your secrets and mine to get it. That hunger for power may be born from mischievousness. He or she might just enjoy making trouble. Or the spy may like the power of knowing something that shouldn't be known or of being the first to know something.

Meagan writes, "I think for some people gossip is like a thrill or a high from being the first one to tell someone else about things. It's like a competition to see who knows the low-down on someone else first. It makes them feel better about themselves because they 'knew' before you did."[5]

Some spies know that they can get something they perceive as better than what they already have by trading one secret for another. We see this often with teenage girls. They trade gossip about each other to maintain power over each other in their cliques. For the spy gossip provides the power to include and exclude.

I'm not immune to this temptation. I like to be known as someone who knows things. I enjoy the feeling and status of being "on the inside." At pastors' gatherings I find myself sharing juicy tidbits about our family of churches, our seminary or some famous Christian I have met—just so that I can be perceived as a "someone." Yuck. I hate to admit this. In this area I need to change.

Incomparably Great Power

If a desire for power is your temptation, then what you really want is Jesus. The power of gossip enslaves, but the power of Christ emancipates. Satan lies about his power, but it was derived from a source other than himself, and it is waning. The devil is a defeated ruler on the way out. Jesus' power, on the other hand, is the power that brought Him back to life after He was crucified, and it is eternal and available through the Holy Spirit of God.

If a desire for power tempts you, then pray along with Paul the prayer of Ephesians 1:

> I pray also that the eyes of your heart may be enlightened in order that you may know the hope to which he has called you, the riches of his glorious inheritance in the saints, *and his incomparably great power for us who believe.* That power is like the working of his mighty strength, which he exerted in Christ when he raised him from the dead and seated him at his right hand in the heavenly realms, far above all rule and authority, power and dominion, and every title that can be given, not only in the present age but also in the one to come. (1:18–21)

That is gospel power, and it is better than anything that gossip promises.

How did Jesus use His power? He used it to love. Jesus was a "trustworthy man," someone to whom you could entrust your deepest, most shameful secrets, and know they were as safe as can be. He still is. And we can learn to be trustworthy too (Prov. 11:13).

Gossip 2: The Grumbler

The other Hebrew word that is commonly translated as "gossip" in the Proverbs is *nirgan*. For example, "A perverse man stirs up dissension, and a gossip [*nirgan*] separates close friends" (Prov. 16:28). The English Standard Version consistently translates *nirgan* as "whisperer." The Hebrew dictionaries say that a *nirgan* is one who is "murmuring about another person behind their back rather than openly complaining about their behavior."[6] The root word for *nirgan* is the same word used to describe the people of Israel when they grumbled in their tents (see Ps. 106:24–25).

Did the Israelites go out and talk directly with the Lord about their concerns? No, they hid in their tents and murmured about Him in secret. (Of course, He heard them; you can't really talk behind the Lord's back. But you get the idea.)

The grumbler complains. He criticizes. When she is upset about something—and misery *loves* company—she will talk about others behind their backs. We often euphemistically call this "venting." Yet there is no constructive purpose in this kind of talk, and no love in the speaker's heart. Just grumbling.

Remember Lynette from the previous chapter? She was a grumbler. She and the other teachers she worked with did not like their supervisor because of bad experiences, so they talked about the supervisor when the supervisor was gone. I believe such a story can be found in just about every workplace in America. And in every family, every city and every school. We love to complain about authority figures, parents, teachers and politicians.

Jealousy

For grumblers jealousy is often a key factor in their motivations. A pastor friend of mine who knew I was studying gossip asked me if jealousy was the root of all gossip. It seemed to him that most if not all of the gossip he encountered came out of a jealous heart. That makes sense, does it not? If you are jealous, you will be tempted to grumble behind the back of someone who has something you want: a job, a girlfriend, a car, happiness or whatever.

"Jason," a friend of mine from church, wrote me a note saying, "About twelve years ago I was discouraged because I saw people in my organization who made more money [than I did] and who I believed did not work as hard or have as hard of a job as I did. Because I felt this way, I would voice my opinion to many people at work."[7]

Can you guess what happened? Two of the people whom Jason was complaining about stopped interacting with him altogether. They wouldn't even say hello to him in the hallway. It took some humbling apologies on Jason's part and a good deal of time before the relationships were restored at all. As we just saw, "A perverse man stirs up dissension, and a gossip [grumbling *nirgan*] separates close friends" (Prov. 16:28).

Content in Any and Every Situation

The gospel remedy for grumbling is contentment and thanksgiving. It is not bad to want something, but it is terribly enslaving to want something too much. As Christians, we need to cultivate a heart of contentment with what we have and of thanksgiving for what we have been given.

Grumbling gossip feels good, even justified and righteous. But it is *not* good. Contentment, however, feels even better. Contentment is counting your blessings and knowing that if you have Jesus Christ, you have everything.

The apostle Paul knew something about contentment. He said, "I know what it is to be in need, and I know what it is to have plenty. I have learned the secret of being content in any and every situation, whether well fed or hungry, whether living in plenty or in want" (Phil. 4:12).

So what was the secret of his contentment? He tells us in the next verse: "I can do everything through [Christ] who gives me strength" (4:13).

That will undo grumbling!

Gossip 3: The Backstabber

Like the grumbler, the backstabber is full of complaint, but his heart is angrier, more hateful. Backstabbing gossip overflows from a heart bent on revenge, retaliation and real malice. The backstabber actually desires the target of his gossip to experience pain.

The backstabber usually begins by spreading lies, starting what we call a "smear campaign." Or a backstabber will hurt someone by simply publishing a shameful truth. Love, on the other hand, covers the warts in another's reputation. Backstabbing not only uncovers the warts but sticks a knife in them.

Absalom was a backstabber. King David's son sat at the gates of Jerusalem and complained about his dad's leadership (see 2 Sam. 15). He told visitors pursuing lawsuits that King David had not appointed enough judges and that justice was not getting done. Absalom did not say this to David, just to the people. He wanted to steal the kingdom from his father, and he almost succeeded.

King David experienced a lot of backstabbing. Remember how he was sick in Psalm 41, and it brought out the gossip of his enemies (we looked at this briefly in chapter 1)? He said, "My enemies say of me *in malice*, 'When will he die and his name perish?' . . . All my enemies whisper together against me; they imagine the worst for me, saying, 'A vile disease has beset him; he will never get up from the place where he lies'" (41:5, 7–8). This is hate.

Here is betrayal: "Even my close friend, whom I trusted, he who shared my bread, has lifted up his heel against me" (41:9). Was David talking about Absalom here? We do not know. But we do know that the Lord Jesus quoted Psalm 41:9 at the Last Supper to refer to Judas Iscariot. Our Lord too knows what it is like to be betrayed.

Malicious gossip, the kind that leads to backstabbing, is the worst kind, because it is the most like Satan's behavior. Hateful gossip tears apart churches. Paul fought it at Corinth (see 2 Cor. 12:20). John dealt with it in his churches (see 3 John 10). Malicious gossip is a cancer. It must be stopped!

Payback

A number of key motivations can be given for backstabbing. Proverbs says, "The purposes of a man's heart are deep waters, but a man of understanding draws them out" (20:5). Motives are often murky and difficult to discern, yet it is possible to wade through them and understand, to some degree, why we do what we do.

For many the water inside the backstabber's heart bottle is the water of revenge. The backstabber has been foiled, perhaps hurt or damaged, and is now angry. He is angry to the point at which he wants someone to pay for what has caused his pain. Gossip becomes a delicious means of payback. The target does not even know what is coming until it is too late.

Backstabbers, however, must beware. Gossip does not satisfy.

It does not always work. Backstabbing often backfires. Wisdom found in Proverbs says, "If a man digs a pit, he will fall into it; if a man rolls a stone, it will roll back on him. A lying tongue hates those it hurts, and a flattering mouth works ruin" (26:27–28).

And what does the gospel say to backstabbers? Certainly more than just "Don't do it! Cut it out! Don't be a hater!" As right as these rebukes might be, they don't go very deep into the heart. The gospel says to the backstabber, "Justice will be done. Leave it in the proper hands" (see Rom. 12:19).

Yes, we should pursue loving confrontation when someone has hurt us. Yes, we should take offenses to the proper authorities. But no, we are not to take revenge. God will see that justice is done. The Bible says,

> Do not take revenge, my friends, but leave room for God's wrath, for it is written: "It is mine to avenge; I will repay," says the Lord. On the contrary: "If your enemy is hungry, feed him; if he is thirsty, give him something to drink. In doing this, you will heap burning coals on his head." Do not be overcome by evil, but overcome evil with good. (Rom. 12:19–21)

Only a Christian can overcome evil with good. We know that every wrong will be repaid either at the cross or in the eternal judgment. Knowing this changes our hearts. It makes it possible for us to not take revenge.

Gossip 4: The Chameleon

A chameleon is a person who goes along with gossip to try to fit into the crowd. A commenter on my blog said, "I think that sometimes people gossip so they can be a part of the conversation. If they know something 'interesting' about another person, they might get people to listen to them."[8] In other words, everybody else is doing it, and we don't want to be left out.

Escaping the Snare

Fear, not anger, is the main motivation for a chameleon's gossip. A chameleon is afraid of what her peers will think, say or do if she does not produce some gossip on demand. She is especially afraid of being excluded.

We can easily scoff at others when they are afraid in this way, but when we are the ones in a similar situation, we find that it is very difficult to resist the pressure. Proverbs says, "Fear of man will prove to be a snare, but whoever trusts in the LORD is kept safe" (29:25).

The key for the chameleon is to trust in the Lord and, even more, to fear Him. The Lord Jesus said, "I tell you, my friends, do not be afraid of those who kill the body and after that can do no more. But I will show you whom you should fear: Fear him who, after the killing of the body, has power to throw you into hell. Yes, I tell you, fear him" (Luke 12:4–5). The answer to the fear of man is the fear of God.

But not a slavish fear. Jesus goes on to say, "Are not five sparrows sold for two pennies? Yet not one of them is forgotten by God. Indeed, the very hairs of your head are all numbered. Don't be afraid; you are worth more than many sparrows" (12:6–7). The fear of God brings peace and comfort.

Imagine a chameleon-type person hanging around with Lynette in her teachers' lounge. She has always participated in dishing out gossip because she is afraid of being excluded by the other teachers. Let's imagine, however, that her mind becomes more and more full of God's character. His holiness. His omnipotence. His faithfulness. His awesomeness. And let's imagine further that she reminds herself that her hairs are all numbered and that God truly cares for her.

If God looms in her mind and heart like that, her coworkers' opinions and snarky comments will shrink in importance, and the chameleon will begin to stand out as a follower of Christ.

Gossip 5: The Busybody

The busybody is a person who is idle, not engaged in purposeful business and wants to be entertained. He gossips for titillation and for the purpose of living vicariously through the stories of others. A busybody enjoys meddling in other people's business. Paul says, "They are not busy; they are busybodies" (2 Thess. 3:11).

It is easy to fall into this kind of behavior. In First Timothy 5 Paul explained to Timothy what to do about widows. The church in Ephesus had a list of widows whom they supported. A widow had to meet certain qualifications to be put on this list. Most of the qualifications were about godliness, but to be added to the list, a woman also had to be an older widow, because younger widows would be prone to particular temptations if they were put on a list like this when they were too young. Paul told Timothy, "They get into the habit of being idle and going about from house to house. And not only do they become idlers, but also gossips and busybodies, saying things they ought not to" (1 Tim. 5:13).

Let's be clear: this behavior is *not* just a female thing! Women get blamed for being gossips more than men do because they are more relational by nature and more interested in the things that make up stereotypical gossip. Gossip, though, is a gender-equal sin. The busybodies Paul confronted in Thessalonica included a number of unemployed *men* (see 2 Thess 3:6-14). If we are not busy with productive, purposeful, godly activity, any of us can easily be sucked into being a gossipy busybody.

Being a busybody gets us into trouble, especially when we get involved in people's conflicts. Proverbs says, "Like one who seizes a dog by the ears is a passer-by who meddles in a quarrel not his own" (26:17). I wouldn't want to try grabbing the ears of the big barking dogs in my neighborhood, so why would I insert myself and my unsolicited opinions into someone else's problem? Is it because I am lacking something good to do?

Escape from Boredom

Our culture encourages it all: gossip columns, gossip shows on television and gossip blogs with the latest story about whichever celebrity is popular this moment. Gossip is big business in show business. The entertainment industry has tapped into the desire of the masses to escape from boredom. We talk about other people to have something to do.

Can you relate? I know that I can certainly be a busybody when I'm bored. I hate to admit it, but I was hooked on soap operas when I was a teenager. I had to watch *General Hospital* before I went out on my after-school paper route. What is that except a malignant desire to be entertained by bad stories?

We rationalize it. "It is not *malicious* gossip," we say. And that is true. But it isn't *love* either, is it? Remember that the Lord Jesus said we would have to give an account "for every *careless* word" (Matt. 12:36), not just the malicious ones.

I have a new slogan that I have been preaching to myself recently:

The foolish people of the world do not exist for my entertainment.

That is a hard one to accept. We love to talk about the foolish, shameful things that people do. There are many places on the Internet that are devoted to laughing at the folly of others. Isn't that the point of most of the "reality" shows on television? It makes us feel good about ourselves to think how stupid other people are.

But that isn't how God treats people, is it? God loves people and treats them with much more mercy than they deserve. God loves me, and I have been a fool. But God, in love, sent His own Son to die for fools in order to make us wise.

The "gospel escape" from boredom is active love, active service and active mercy for other people—including those who do not deserve it one bit. Paul tells the young widows to marry and to have children (see 1 Tim. 5:14). Marriage and motherhood are not an antidote to gossip, but they sure can be an antidote to idleness! Paul told the busybody men in the church in Thessalonica to get a job, and if they were not willing to do so, they were not to eat. And the rest of the church was to warn them and keep away from them (see 2 Thess. 3:10–15; also 1 Thess. 5:14).

If we reach out to others in love, we will never be bored. Tired? Yes. Bored? No.

The People that You Meet

So these are some of the people in our neighborhood: the spy, the grumbler, the backstabber, the chameleon and the busybody. Recognize them? We have run into all of them at one time or another—and have been most of them too! These people might act differently from one another, but at heart, they are all the same. Each one is moved by a heart that believes Satan's original lie, loves a bad story and worships something that is not God. Each one has gotten everything backwards. Each one uses words to selfishly serve himself or herself rather than to love God and love other people (see Luke 10:27).

But our gracious God speaks to each of these hearts with His life-changing gospel truth, and He is speaking to each one of us right now (see Heb. 3:7–13). Are we listening?

Looking Ahead

We are about to head into part 2, where we are going to get specific about how to go about resisting gossip. The first step will be to recognize one more gossiping kind of person, who, sadly, lives inside of each one of us: the judge.

Questions for Group Discussion

1. Chapter 3 says that in the Bible gossip is more about people than about their words. How is this so? Why is that important for us to understand?

2. Which of the five kinds of gossips are you most prone to be? Which of them have you encountered recently "in your neighborhood"? (Remember: do not fall into gossiping about others while discussing how to resist gossip!)

3. Read Proverbs 20:5. Pick two or three of the following kinds of gossips and discuss the motivations of each one at the heart level. What other motivations would you add?

    a. The spy: a lust for power

    b. The grumbler: jealousy

    c. The backstabber: a desire for revenge

d. The chameleon: the fear of man

e. The busybody: escape from boredom

4. Take the same list and discuss the biblical truths listed below that speak to each hijacked heart. What other gospel truths would you add?

   a. The spy: Ephesians 1:18–21

   b. The grumbler: Philippians 4:12–13

   c. The backstabber: Romans 12:19–21

   d. The chameleon: Proverbs 29:25; Luke 12:4–7

   e. The busybody: 2 Thessalonians 3:10–15

5. Change is not automatic. Simply reading a Bible verse does not fix our hearts. What can we do to internalize the truths we've just learned so that God can use them to transform us? What are you going to do about that this week?

PART 2
Resisting Gossip

There is only one Lawgiver and Judge, the one who is able to save and destroy. But you—who are you to judge your neighbor?

James 4:12

4

Believing the Best

How embarrassing!
I hung up the phone and hung my head, a deep red blush covering my face. I could not believe that I had done it. I was the guy who was writing a book on resisting gossip, and *look what I'd just done.*

Half an hour before I'd taken a call from "Ethan," a man I had once known but had not talked to in a long while. He and his new girlfriend were having trouble in their relationship and wanted some counsel from a pastor. I tried to help him some over the phone, but honestly, I didn't have much hope in their ability to work things out. I thought they had made too many bad choices leading up to their present difficulties, including moving in together before marriage.

But they *had not* moved in together. I'd just assumed it.

And when I mentioned it as a problem in their relationship, I heard an awkward pause on the other end of the line.

"Matt," Ethan declared, "we aren't living together! I wouldn't do that." Ethan went on to explain the pains that he went through daily to make sure that as a couple he and his girlfriend stayed chaste and above reproach. As I said, I was so embarrassed.

"I am so sorry, Ethan."

"It's okay, Matt. Probably other people think the same thing too. It's normal in our world today."

"But, I am really sorry, Ethan. I shouldn't have assumed."

Even worse, after I apologized a third time and got off the phone, I started to mentally list the names of the people to whom I had errantly affirmed that Ethan and his girlfriend were living together. Gossip.

Sinful Judgments

Most, if not all, sinful gossip includes the sin of judging others. When we sinfully gossip, then even before we go and bear bad news behind someone's back, our bad hearts have already passed sentence upon that person. This is true no matter what kind of gossiper we are.

The spy tries to get people to feel judgmental enough to wangle a secret out of them. The grumbler has decided in his heart that the person he is talking about is clearly wrong and merits a complaint, at least, and probably a much stronger denunciation. The backstabber is certain of her judgment and knows that her target deserves the retaliation that is on the way. The chameleon listens in on the judgments of others and does not speak up for fear of reprisal. The busybody escapes from boredom by issuing entertaining but condemning judgments about other people to his or her friends. Busybodies snicker at those they judge to be "the stupid people."

The connection between sinful judging and sinful gossip is clearly seen in the book of James:

> Brothers, do not slander one another. Anyone who speaks against his brother or judges him speaks against the law and judges it. When you judge the law, you are not keeping it,

but sitting in judgment on it. There is only one Lawgiver and Judge, the one who is able to save and destroy. But you—who are you to judge your neighbor? (4:11–12)

The Greek word translated "slander" in James 4:11 is *katalaleo*, and it means more than just maliciously lying about someone, which is how we tend to define the English word "slander." *Kataleleo* means to speak against someone, to talk them down, to speak ill of them, to disdain someone or to run somebody down verbally. Older versions translate James 4:11 this way: "Speak not evil one of another, brethren" (KJV).

Authors Tim Keller and David Powlison say, "[*Katalaleo*] is not necessarily a false report, just an 'against-report.' The intent is to belittle another. To pour out contempt. To mock. To hurt. To harm. To destroy. To rejoice in purported evil."[1] Sounds a lot like sinful gossip, doesn't it?

Kataleleo appears right next to the chief Greek word for gossip (*psithurismos*) in both Romans 1:30 and Second Corinthians 12:20. *Kataleleo* is the larger category of evil-speaking against someone (sometimes taking secretive forms), and gossip itself is actually a subcategory of the word, meaning to *katalaleo*, or speak against someone, behind that person's back.

James connects *kataleleo* to sinful judging. He says, as we read above, "Brothers, do not slander [run down, disdain, gossip about] one another." Why? He goes on: "Anyone who speaks against [*katalaleo* again] his brother or *judges him* speaks against the law and judges it." When we speak against someone in this way, James says that we are sinfully judging that person.

I said "*sinfully* judging," because not all judging is sinful (just as not all small talk is sinful gossip). We have to make judgments all the time. We are called upon to make decisions about other people, to assess their character and reliability. The Bible calls for us to be discerning people who use good judgment. Author Ken Sande says that "judging is necessary but dangerous."[2]

But there is an unnecessary kind of judging that leads to sinful gossip. This is the kind of judging that Jesus talked about when he said, "Do not judge, or you too will be judged" (Matt 7:1). We call this kind of judging "judgmental," as it is more of an attitude. It's a heart disposition meant to be condemnatory and censorious.

Where do we go wrong with judging? Let's consider three main ways.

1. Rush to Judgment

I formed a conclusion about Ethan before I had all the facts about his situation. That is easy to do. Proverbs says, "He who answers before listening—that is his folly and his shame" (18:13). I sure felt ashamed and foolish with Ethan. I like to joke that I get all my exercise by pushing my luck and jumping to conclusions. Yet joking aside, it is important for followers of Christ not to jump to conclusions.

Listening to Only One Side

Much of gossip is simply passing on one side of a story. A pastor out West wrote to me about a gossip situation in his local church. A woman had stood up one Sunday and requested prayer for a young lady ("Emily") in their tight-knit community. She said that Emily had been kicked out of her home by her parents, and in desperation she had moved in with her boyfriend. Everyone in the church felt sorry for Emily and started to pray for her. But that is not all there was to the story.

Proverbs says, "The first to present his case seems right, till another comes forward and questions him" (18:17). Yet we say, "Well, I can't exactly wait *forever* and talk with *everyone* before making a judgment!"

Actually, we can. We can *suspend judgment* until we have more facts. Or, at the very least, we can make a provisional judgment until we get the other side of the story. And if we do not get more of the facts, unless we are directly involved in the problem, most of the time we can live without knowing the full story.

The truth in Emily's case was that she had left home because she wanted to live with her boyfriend, and her father had no legal recourse, because Emily, a senior in high school, was of age. Her dad badly wanted his daughter back and was deeply grieved by the circumstances.

The pastor wrote:

> The well-meaning lady who asked for prayer was deceived by her daughter-in-law, who had helped this eighteen-year-old leave and had "covered her reputation" by inventing this outrageous lie. The members of our church spread the story before I knew enough to debunk it, and right now dozens, perhaps hundreds, of people have the wrong idea about the father in question, a local leader well known previously for integrity. Of course, the false allegation has hurt him badly, and recovery, if possible, remains a long way off. The church people were told by me and the lady that the story was false, but the damage was done. The fire started and cannot be put out. [Emily] is now caught by the same lie, and her path to return home is now that much more difficult."[3]

Before judging, get both sides.

Not Considering the Source

Hearsay and secondhand information must be treated with the utmost care. Filling in the gaps of a story through guesswork and speculation will get us into trouble really quickly. Questionable sources of information should be treated like hot uranium.

For example, beware of anything that comes to your inbox with these three letters in front of it: Fwd. Just because something is on the Internet does not make it true. Sure, that should be obvious, but how many times have well-meaning people believed something they read in an anonymous (or spuriously attributed) e-mail and then gullibly passed it on?

Proverbs says, "A simple man believes anything, but a prudent man gives thought to his steps" (14:15). Do not believe everything you hear!

Assuming Motives

You and I are not mind readers. We cannot see inside the hearts of other people and know exactly what makes them tick. Only God can do that (see 1 Sam. 16:7). Therefore, we need to assume the best, not the worst, about others' motives whenever possible. Unless someone tells us what motivates them or it has become obvious through a "pattern of incontrovertible facts that can lead to no other reasonable conclusion,"[4] we need to assume the best.

Assuming motives almost plunged Israel into civil war on one occasion. We read in Joshua 22 that after the nation had finally experienced victory and gained rest from their enemies, three of the tribes, Reuben, Gad and Manasseh, went back over the river to their previously agreed-upon home in Gilead. The next thing they did was erect an "imposing altar" on their side of the Jordan (see 22:10).

The other tribes assembled at Shiloh to wage war. Why? They assumed that the Transjordan tribes were setting up their own sacrificial system to rival the one in Israel. Israel had already experienced the pain of God's discipline for allowing false worship in the past. They were not going to let that happen again so soon.

Thankfully, they sent a team across the river first to try to stop the Transjordan tribes by diplomatic means. In that heated conference it came out that the tribes of Reuben, Gad and Manasseh had only built the altar as a symbol of witness reminding both sides of their common Lord! Disaster was averted when their true motives came out.

What situations are *you* tempted to gossip about right now? Do you truly know the motives of those involved? Sometimes things *seem* obvious. After all, we read in Joshua 22 that there was a humongous altar standing on the riverbank! But there may be another explanation for the things that we see.

Are We Supposed to Be Ostriches?

Believing the best about someone's motives does not mean that we put our heads in the sand and pretend that nothing bad is happening. No, we have to call sin, sin. But we should also hold out hope for people and not assume the worst about them. That is what sinful judging is at heart: assuming the worst about people.

As Christians, it would seem that we have more reason to assume the worst about people than most. We have the doctrine of sin. We know that people often have bad motives and do bad things. But also as Christians, we are called to hold out hope for people and not to assign bad motives to them until we have to. The Bible says, "Judge nothing before the appointed time;

wait till the Lord comes. He will bring to light what is hidden in darkness and will expose the motives of men's hearts" (1 Cor. 4:5). Let's wait for Him.

If we are slower to judge others and stop sharing our judgments, how much gossip will that cut out?

2. Prideful Judgment

It gets worse. Our problem with sinful judging goes deeper than just rushing to judgment. James identifies our deeper problem as pride.

He says, "Anyone who speaks against his brother or judges him speaks against the law and judges it. When you judge the law, you are not keeping it, but sitting in judgment on it" (James 4:11). To give some context, the law James is talking about is the law of love, the royal law of mercy that God calls His people to obey (see 2:8). But when you and I sinfully judge someone, we are saying, in effect, that we are above the law. We are saying that the law does not apply to us and that we can judge *it*. That is not the way it works.

James goes on: "There is only one Lawgiver and Judge, the one who is able to save and destroy. But you—who are you to judge your neighbor?" (4:12). When we find ourselves sinfully judging, we are essentially playing God. Who do we think we are?

Is This My Place?

The Lord calls us to be the servants of others, but we are tempted to act as if we are their judges. Instead, when we get into these kinds of situations, we should regularly ask ourselves questions like these:

- Is this my place?

- Is this my job?
- Am I part of this situation? What part?
- Is judging this person my calling, my responsibility?

If the answers are no, then we need to cut it out.

Of course, there are positions in life in which we are temporarily required to serve as a judge. Parents have to serve as judges at times, as do teachers, coaches and church leaders. Most earthly positions of authority come with a limited responsibility to adjudicate something.

But even in those cases, we *serve* as judges. We do not play God and make up our own standard, and we do not pretend that we would *never* do what another person has done. That's one of the worst forms of judging—acting as if we ourselves have never done anything as wrong as what someone else has done, anything similarly foolish or anything every bit as worthy of condemnation. God knows better. The Lord Jesus says that we need to apply the same standard to ourselves as we do to those we are tempted to judge, because God will.

> Do not judge, or you too will be judged. For in the same way you judge others, you will be judged, and with the measure you use, it will be measured to you. Why do you look at the speck of sawdust in your brother's eye and pay no attention to the plank in your own eye? How can you say to your brother, "Let me take the speck out of your eye," when all the time there is a plank in your own eye? You hypocrite, first take the plank out of your own eye, and then you will see clearly to remove the speck from your brother's eye. (Matt. 7:1–5)

This passage has always reminded me of *The Three Stooges*. Jesus is saying there is a telephone pole sticking out of Moe's eye socket, but Moe is intent on getting a dust mote out of Larry's eye! In the end, somebody is going to get walloped.

That's what happens when we presume to play God. With a rush to judgment, we act as if we are omniscient when we are not. With pride in our judgment, we act as if we are perfectly objective when we most certainly are not!

In the Same Way You Judge Others

How often do the Republicans judge what is wrong with the Democrats but give their party a pass when it comes to what is wrong with them? And vice versa! Democrats find fault with Republicans over everything, yet they do not criticize their own party. It is pride when we pick and choose what is most wrong about another based upon our own self-exaltation. We all are prone to do this.

Here is where Jesus' Golden "Rule of Thumb" is so golden. The Lord says, "So in everything, do to others what you would have them do to you, for this sums up the Law and the Prophets" (Matt. 7:12). Given this command, we should consider the following:

1. How would *you* have others judge you?
2. With what standard?
3. With what tone?
4. With what attitude would you want to be judged?

Once you have your answers, then choose that standard, that tone and that attitude when making your judgments. Use that standard when you are talking about people who are not present.

I read the following little story in an e-mail. I doubt that it is true (it was marked "Fwd," after all), but it makes a good point.

A young couple moved into a new neighborhood. The next morning while they were eating breakfast, the young woman saw her neighbor hanging the wash outside.

"That laundry is not very clean," she said. "She doesn't know how to wash correctly. Perhaps she needs better laundry soap."

Her husband looked on, but remained silent. Every time her neighbor would hang her wash to dry, the young woman would make the same comments.

About one month later, the woman was surprised to see a nice clean wash on the line and said to her husband, "Look, she has learned how to wash correctly. I wonder who taught her this."

The husband said, "I got up early this morning and cleaned our windows."

The e-mail ends, "And so it is with life. What we see when watching others depends on the window through which we look." How true! Proverbs says, "A man who lacks judgment derides his neighbor, but a man of understanding holds his tongue" (11:12).

Humble Yourself

The antidote to prideful judgment is humility. In the verse right before James' condemnation of slander and judging, he says, "Humble yourselves before the Lord, and he will lift you up" (4:10). We need to judge our judgments, check our motives and remember our place.

3. Unloving Judgment

Another name for sinful judging is critical judgment. The opposite virtue is called charitable judgment. The word "charitable" comes from the old word for love, which is charity, and it is beautifully described in First Corinthians 13:

> Love [charity] is patient, love is kind. It does not envy, it does not boast, it is not proud. It is not rude, it is not self-seeking, it is not easily angered, it keeps no record of wrongs. Love does not delight in evil but rejoices with the truth. It always protects, always trusts, always hopes, always perseveres. Love never fails. (1 Cor. 13:4–8)

If you and I are loving people with this kind of charity, we won't sinfully judge or gossip about people. We won't delight in the evil that we hear has befallen someone else. We won't believe the worst about others. We will always hope for something better. Love is tenacious. Love does not pretend that all is well and sweep things under the carpet, but it does hang onto hope for others and believe the best.

This is how Jesus loved us, isn't it? Substitute the name "Jesus" for the word "love" in First Corinthians 13 to see the greatest example of "the most excellent way" (1 Cor. 12:31).

Can you imagine Jesus gossiping about us? He would surely be fully qualified to do so. He knows the whole truth about us and *could* rush to judgment. He *is* the lawgiver and the judge. Yet Jesus is patient and kind. Jesus does not delight in evil. He does not sinfully judge us. He saved us by His own sacrificial death. If Jesus has shown us this love, we need to show it to others.

Looking Ahead

Of course, it is not enough when it comes to judgmental gossip to just tell ourselves, "Cut it out!" We must learn how to do that. What do we do instead? In the next two chapters, let's consider biblical alternatives to sinful gossip, first in speaking and then in listening.

Questions for Group Discussion

1. Read James 4:10–12. What is the connection between sinful judging and gossip?
2. What are the differences between being judgmental (sinful judging) and being discerning (righteous judgment)? How do we know when we are doing the wrong one?
3. Read the following proverbs and discuss the wisdom given in each of them for not rushing into judgment. Can you give an example from your life (positive or negative) for each one?

    a. Proverbs 14:15

    b. Proverbs 18:13

    c. Proverbs 18:17

4. Read Matthew 7:1–5. How does pride distort our judgment? How can we cultivate humility? How can we cultivate love?
5. Read First Corinthians 13:4–8. Think of a current relationship of yours in which you have been prone to sinful judging. What would loving that person look like this week?

Do not let any unwholesome talk come out of your mouths, but only what is helpful for building others up according to their needs, that it may benefit those who listen.

Ephesians 4:29

5

Instead of Gossip: Speaking

I wish I had a dime for every time I've heard someone say, "But if we didn't gossip, we wouldn't have anything to talk about!" Of course that is not true. But it often *feels* as if it is.

If you are like me, you do not *want* to gossip. Sure, you feel like gossiping sometimes, but your basic stance is against it. You do not *want* to be a gossipmonger. After all, you are reading a book about resisting gossip! But gossiping often *feels* irresistible. It is hard to see any alternative.

What do we do instead of gossiping?

The good news is that God wants to help us. The Lord does not want us to just stop our sinful behavior. He wants us to live righteously. And He gives us, practically, everything we need to do just that.

Stinky Words

In Ephesians 4 God instructs us through the apostle Paul. He says, "Do not let any unwholesome talk come out of your mouths, but only what is helpful for building others up according to their needs, that it may benefit those who listen" (4:29).

The Greek word translated "unwholesome" is *sapros*. It means something rotten, corrupt or decomposed. *Sapros* was used to talk about fruit that had gone bad and fish that had begun to stink.[1] So words that are *sapros* are rotten words. Yucky words. Words gone bad. Stinky bad news. Gossip is not the only kind of talk that fits into that category, but it is definitely in there.

Notice that Paul does not just call on the Ephesians to refrain from rotten words, but he also instructed them *instead* to use their words to bless others. Overcoming gossip is not just about what *not* to do but what *to* do.

Become Who You Are

To really understand Ephesians 4:29 (and especially to live it out), we have to understand it in its context. In the first three chapters of Ephesians, the apostle Paul explains the gospel as God's amazing eternal plan to bring glory to Himself through Christ. Then Paul turns a corner and applies the gospel. So in the last three chapters of the book, he explains the implications of the gospel worked out in our lives: in a word, *change*. The truth of the gospel transforms us so that now we can live differently.

Before Christ we lived one way. We were "darkened in [our] understanding and separated from the life of God because of the ignorance that is in [us] due to the hardening of [our] hearts. Having lost all sensitivity, [we gave] [our]selves over to sensuality so as to indulge in every kind of impurity, with a continual lust for more" (Eph. 4:18–19). That sounds like the addictive quality of gossip, doesn't it? "A continual lust" for more of those "choice morsels."

Now we live differently. The next couple of verses explain our transformation: "[We], however, did not come to know

Christ that way. Surely [we] heard of him and were taught in him in accordance with the truth that is in Jesus" (4:20–21). That's the gospel! That's the good news about Jesus Christ and His death and resurrection and the gift of His Spirit and the promise of His return.

Paul goes on to say that we "were taught, with regard to [our] former way of life, to put off [our] old self, which is being corrupted by its deceitful desires; to be made new in the attitude of [our] minds; and to put on the new self, created to be like God in true righteousness and holiness" (4:22–24). He is saying that our new relationship with Jesus through the gospel has changed everything. As a result, we need *to become who we are*. We have a new identity now, and we need to live out of that identity.

Paul likens it to changing clothes. Take off an old coat. Put on a new coat.

The old coat, the old you, has to go. It is "being corrupted by its deceitful desires" (4:22). Instead, we need to "be made new in the attitude of [our] minds" (4:23). That means taking in and believing all the gospel truths we've learned so far. Moreover, we need to "put on the new self, created to be like God in true righteousness and holiness" (4:24). That's the new coat! It's the new you, the real you, the you now in Christ. It is who you really are by grace. But we need to put this new self on.

Paul ran with this idea:

Put off lying. Put on truth-speaking (see 4:25).

Put off sinful anger. Put on peacemaking (see 4:26–27).

Put off stealing. Put on generosity (see 4:28).

Do you see the pattern? Put off. Put on. We could call this repenting and obeying. Doing this comes not through our self-effort but out of our faith in Christ and our new identity in Him.

This is the context for verse 29, which says, "Do not let any unwholesome talk [including rotten gossip] come out of your mouths, but only what is helpful for building others up according to their needs, that it may benefit those who listen."

Put off gossip. Put on up-building speech.

It's not a one-and-done sort of thing. It is an as-often-as-needed sort of thing. Put off. Put on. Again and again and again.

Now let's get *really* practical. What does this look like in real life? Let me suggest five things that we can do instead of speaking gossip—five new coats for us to put on.

1. Say Nothing At All

If you are faced with gossip or the possibility of gossiping, often the best thing to say is nothing. As the saying goes, "If you can't say anything good, don't say anything at all." Silence can be golden.

Proverbs says, "When words are many, sin is not absent, but he who holds his tongue is wise" (10:19). Often discretion is evidenced by silence. Proverbs 17 says, "A man of knowledge uses words with restraint, and a man of understanding is even-tempered. Even a fool is thought wise if he keeps silent, and discerning if he holds his tongue" (17:27–28).

Abraham Lincoln put it this way: "It is better to keep your mouth shut and let them think you are a fool than to open your mouth and remove all doubt."[2] This rule of thumb goes not just for face-to-face talking but also for texting, messaging, e-mailing and every other kind of communication through which gossip could flow.

Secrets

When I was teaching about resisting gossip at church, one of our members asked me an insightful question.

> Is it gossip if someone confides in you about something and asks you not to tell anyone but to pray for them? You in turn have a Christian friend, a prayer warrior, whom you trust would never repeat anything you tell them. Is it gossip if I repeat what someone confides in me to my Christian friend only for them to pray about the situation?[3]

If someone asks you not to share something with anyone but just to pray, then you should not tell anyone and just pray. Remember, "A gossip betrays a confidence, but a trustworthy man keeps a secret" (Prov. 11:13). You certainly could ask your prayer-requesting friend if you can share the secret with a safe prayer warrior who has your absolute trust, but do not do it if you have been asked not to.

I had a similar problem when I was writing this chapter. I learned of a really scandalous secret, and I wanted so much to tell someone. Not someone involved—just someone, anyone! But I held my tongue and will continue to do so, because I want to be a trustworthy man.

There are exceptions, of course. For example, the case of someone being significantly harmed by keeping a secret such as a suicidal threat. This kind of information clearly should be revealed to those who can help. In fact, no secret is absolute if it will damage someone. However, most of the time, silence is golden. Paul says that "only what is helpful" should be shared. Nothing more.

2. Commend the Commendable

Often we can do even better than silence. We can say something good. Ephesians 4:29 also tells us to speak words that are "helpful for building others up." That means offering encouragement, commendation, affirmation and approving words. If we are tempted to talk about someone, then we should talk about that person's good points.

The next time you are tempted to gossip about someone, talk about how good that individual is. That is what Jesus' Golden Rule implies. Speak about people in the way you would want them to speak about you.

Commending Instead of Complaining

Have you ever heard a kid complain about her mom and dad behind their backs? She may say, "My dad never lets me do anything," or, "My mom never gives me anything." In most cases these kinds of complaints are gossip. Instead, kids could and should honor their father and mother by saying things like, "My dad takes me places," "My mom is kind to me," "My dad is the best mechanic," "My mom makes the best meals," or, "My dad is so funny. He makes me laugh" (see Eph. 6:2).

We adults can do that about our moms and dads too, even if we are older. We can also commend our coworkers, fellow church members and neighbors even if most of the time they get on our nerves.

So if there is absolutely nothing good to say about a person, do not say anything; but if there is something, anything, then let's hear *that*. Build people up when they are not around. Bear *good news* about people instead of bad.

Aren't we all attracted to people who build others up? Not people who pretend that everyone is good all the time—that's false and rotten itself. Not people who flatter others—that's false too. But people who choose not to tear others down. These people are extremely appealing. We want to be around them. We want to be like them.

Those who constantly complain, however, are revolting. A

faraway friend of mine sent me a screen capture of the Facebook page of a wife who was complaining about her husband to her friends. I guess you could say it was not technically "behind his back," because her husband probably had access to it himself, but it definitely did not build him up. It tore him down. My faraway friend asked if this was sinful gossip, and I had to say, "Yes, I think so. I'm glad she's not *my* wife."

I don't often complain about my wife, because there is just so little to complain about with Heather Joy. She is, like Mary Poppins, "practically perfect in every way." But I know that I've been guilty of complaining *to* her about other people.

One night early in our marriage, one of our family members came to stay overnight at our apartment, and during her visit I got irritated about something she did. I don't remember what. In our bedroom that night, I complained long and hard to Heather Joy about our relative. However, it turns out that our relative could hear me through the doors and the walls. Oops! It was summer at the time, but it was chilly at our place the next morning!

Now how different would that situation have been if I had put off the old coat of complaining and put on up-building talk?

Edify, Stupid!

The old word for up-building talk is "edification." It is too bad that we've lost that word, because it communicates something powerful: our words can make someone feel as solid as a house or decimate a person the way a wrecking ball could. In Bible college my friends and I used to jokingly bid each other, "Edify, stupid!" It was our humorous way of reminding ourselves of the potency of our words.

Edification does not mean that we commend the *un*-commendable. That's lying. Just find out what you can say that's positive and then build up from there. Need a few ideas? I got the phrase "commend the commendable" from Sam Crabtree's book *Practicing Affirmation*. In chapter 9 "100 Affirmation Ideas for Those Who Feel Stuck," Crabtree offers a great list of options.[4] That gives us a start! The bottom line? Because of our new identity in Christ, it is very possible to say good things about people!

3. Talk *to* People, Not *about* Them

When there is a problem between us and another person, the overwhelming temptation for us is to run to just about anybody other than the one with whom we have the conflict. The way forward in conflict, however, is not to talk *about* the other person but to talk *to* the person in love. Jesus says, "First go and be reconciled to your brother" (Matt. 5:24).

Sometimes that's really hard to do. Yet remember, the new you that you are putting on is greater and stronger and more real than the old you. You can do it! Put off gossip, and put on loving confrontation.

Did someone offend you at church? Talk to him about it. Did a coworker hurt your feelings in a meeting? Bring it up with her. Did your parents' recent decision mess up your plans? Take it up with them.

We need to teach this kind of loving confrontation to our kids. Does the following conversation sound familiar?

> Child: "Little Johnny hit me!" (Bearing bad news behind Johnny's back.)
> Mommy: "Why are you telling me this?" (Out of a bad heart?)
> Child: "To get him in trouble!" (Yep. Out of a bad heart.)
> Mommy: "You need to go talk with *Johnny* about that. If you can't resolve it, *then* I'll get involved."

We all need to practice loving confrontation. As we've seen, Paul says that we should only speak "what is helpful for building others up *according to their needs.*" Sometimes what people really need is loving confrontation.

I know I do. That's why God has given me Heather Joy. I would be in such a mess if she did not wisely and lovingly rebuke me often. The other day Heather Joy pointed out how grouchy I had been recently with our kids. The kids were beginning to avoid me out of fear that I would overreact when disciplining them. I needed to hear that from her, but I'm awfully glad that she did not also run around to her girlfriends to confess my sins to them!

Amy Carmichael, missionary to India in the late nineteenth and early twentieth centuries, had this rule for managing conflicts at her mission station: "Never *about*, always *to*."[5] Conflicts are fanned into flame when we talk about people, but they can be resolved when we talk directly to the person with whom we have the problem.

I should note that it is not gossip to report a crime to the police or an unresolved conflict to your pastor or your elders. It is not gossip to get your parents involved in a situation if you do not know how to say something to a friend or if a conversation with the person who hurt you is not going well. But the general rule is "Never about, always to."

Exception: Warnings

As we said in chapter 1, there are times when we *have* to talk about someone else and tell people about bad things in order to warn others. Warning others is a biblical principle, and not all loving warnings will be issued in front of the subject's face. In fact, they often will not be.

We still, however, have to love a person even when we are warning someone else about them. While warning, we need to do everything we can to protect the person's reputation as much as possible with as much fairness and charitable judgment as we can. Again, that is what we would want others to do for us, isn't it?

One time my friend John had to warn his friend "Ryan" about a mutual acquaintance. John had access to some seemingly credible evidence that "Michael" was doing drugs. And Michael wanted to date Ryan's teenage daughter. John felt terrible about telling the story to Ryan, but he wanted to protect Ryan's family. It wasn't out of a bad heart that John bore bad news. John told Ryan everything he knew, but he also stressed it might turn out to be a misunderstanding and that his personal experience with Michael had been all good. I don't believe that John was gossiping. He was warning in love.

Of course, we can justify just about anything, so we definitely need to make sure our warnings are necessary. We also need to make sure that they demonstrate love toward all the parties concerned. It does not mean that all the parties will be happy that we shared the warning! But our consciences can be clean if we have loved as we would want to be loved.

4. Offer Words of Mercy

Our key verse for this chapter, Ephesians 4:29, ends by saying that our words should build up others "according to their needs, *that it may benefit those who listen*." The King James Version expresses the Greek even better: it says to use words that "may minister grace unto the hearers."

Don't you just love people who dispense grace like it's going out of style? People like that are putting on their new coat in Jesus. They "get" who they are in Christ, and they are so much fun to be around. Proverbs says, "The lips of the righteous nourish many" (10:21). Doesn't that sound good?

I have a friend who is that kind of person. Dan always has something good to say, even when there is not much good to talk about. He's not afraid to confront someone in love when they are offensive, but he goes above and beyond the call of duty and encourages the people he's confronting! He's the first person I call when I have a problem, not just because he is wise but because he is *nourishing*. He uses *merciful* words, and people love to be around him. Dan is what I call "a party waiting to happen," because he's so full of grace.

You and I don't have to say everything we think. In fact, we can be merciful because our heavenly Father is *merciful* (see Luke 6:36). Often we can do better than just staying quiet or even commending the commendable. We can go the extra mile and speak words of grace.

That's what God does, isn't it? Let's be like Him! Remember, Paul said that we need to "put on the new self, created to be *like God* in true righteousness and holiness" (Eph. 4:24). That means that in a potential gossip situation, we should choose the most merciful, most gracious thing we can think of to say. It will take imagination. Righteous living takes more imagination than wicked living, because it doesn't come naturally to us. But it is so much better!

If you are really creative, there are many options for beneficial words. Instead of gossiping, you could:

- Tell a good story,
- Teach something useful,
- Tell a funny joke,

- Talk about the weather,
- Share a joy of yours,
- Or share a loving concern for someone so that you can help him or her.

Whatever you do, say something that "benefit[s] those who listen."

Hard-edged Words

Here's another truth: our words are not always going to be *nice*. Paul is not urging "niceness" upon us. I'm sure that Paul took his own advice when he wrote his letters, yet his epistles certainly contain some words that are much harder-edged than any I have ever spoken. At points Paul even uses ridicule, irony, satire and name-calling!

This certainly does not mean that Paul, in his scriptural writings, violates Ephesians 4:29. There must be ways to obey Ephesians 4:29 and still use remedial words that do not immediately strike somebody as edifying. (Remembering this might help to keep us from falling into the sin of judging others who don't talk just as we think they should.)

The key, I think, is that Paul never used those hard-edged words for his own pleasure or for personal gain. Back to the condition of the heart again! He did not use hard-edged words for the kick of it. Paul always used those words for God, for the gospel, for the good of the church and even for his opponents—to shake them out of their complacency and hard-heartedness.

For us, though, Ephesians 4:29 is simple to apply most of the time. Simple but not easy. And *possible*, because of our new identity in Christ. Remember, let's put off the old coat of gossip and put on the new coat of mercy-giving speech.

5. Talk to and about the Lord

Finally, in Ephesians 5, Paul exhorts us to "speak to one another with psalms, hymns and spiritual songs. Sing and make music in your heart to the Lord, always giving thanks to God the Father for everything, in the name of our Lord Jesus Christ" (5:19–20). When all else fails, we can always use our words to glorify the Lord. Instead of gossiping we can talk to each other, sing to one another, give thanks, share a testimony, pray and worship with our mouths.

If the person we are talking to does not know the Lord yet, even better. One of my professors from seminary used to tell us students to be "gossiping the gospel" wherever we go. The gospel is news that is too good to keep to ourselves!

Looking Ahead

Putting off sinful gossip and putting on grace-giving, people-building, truth-loving, God-imitating, Jesus-like speech is only one side of the coin. What can we do when someone is trying to gossip *to* us? We will look at that in the next chapter.

Questions for Group Discussion

1. Have you ever said, "But if we didn't gossip, we wouldn't have anything to talk about!" Why? Have you ever felt as if gossiping were your only option? When? Where? Why?

2. Read Ephesians 4:17–32. What does it mean to "become who you are"? Why is doing this important for resisting gossip?

3. Read Ephesians 4:29 again, and pick it apart as a group. What are the biblical guidelines of edifying speech?

4. Discuss the five alternatives to speaking gossip that are suggested in this chapter. Which of these might be helpful to you soon? Which do you find hardest to practice? Why? What would you add to the list?

    a. Say nothing at all.

    b. Commend the commendable.

    c. Talk *to* people, not *about* them.

    d. Offer words of mercy.

    e. Talk to and about the Lord.

5. Name someone who is a good example of a person who lives Ephesians 4:29. Tell the group about him or her.

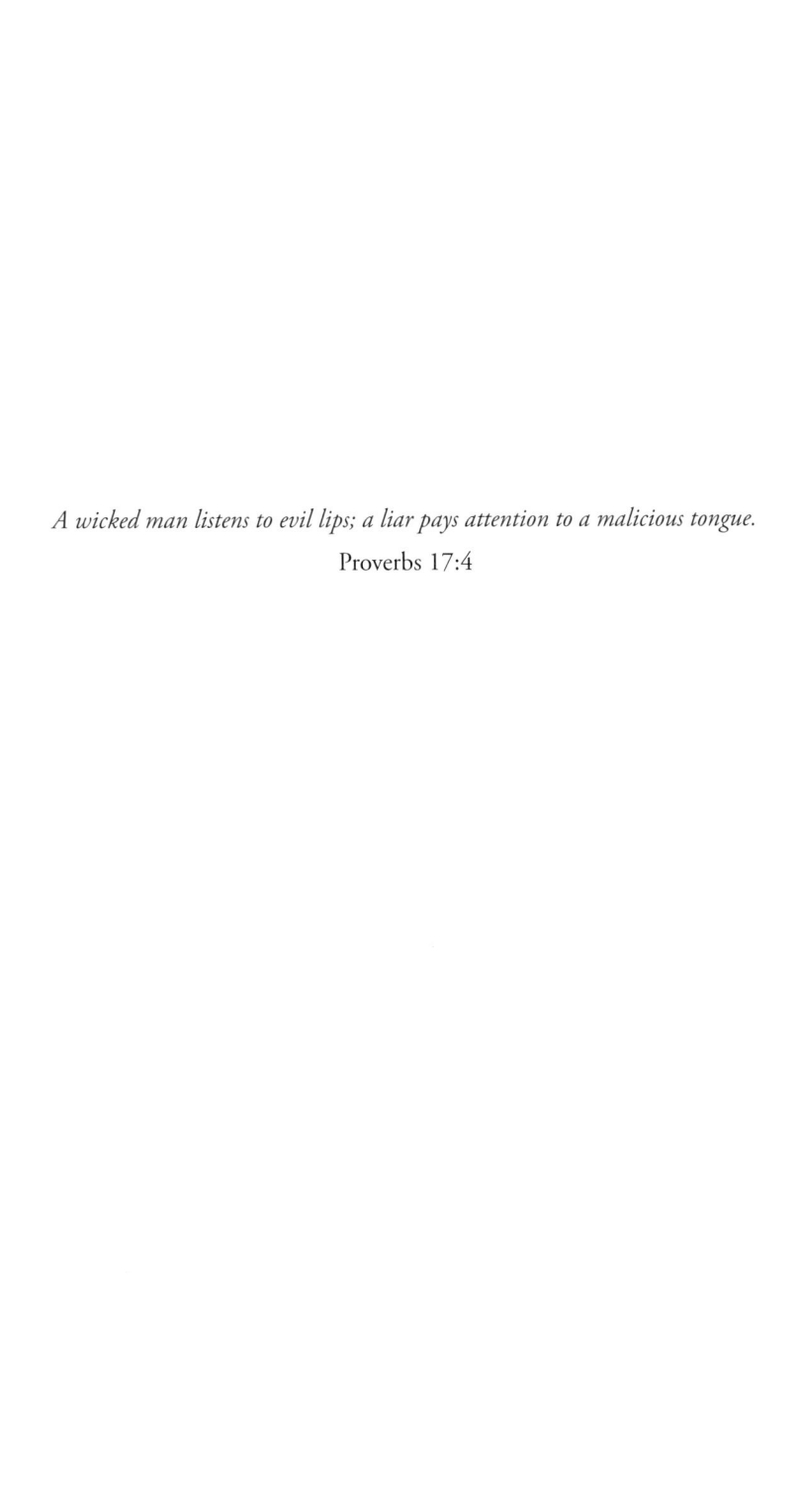

A wicked man listens to evil lips; a liar pays attention to a malicious tongue.
Proverbs 17:4

6

Instead of Gossip: Listening

"It's like they don't have anything else to do but gossip!"

My friend "Natalie" felt trapped. A few months earlier she had begun working as a nurse in a rehab center and was generally enjoying her new job, especially her work with the patients. Her coworkers, however, seemed to be addicted to gossip.

"They take any chance to talk about other people and talk them down. It's hard to escape. What am I supposed to do?"

Natalie told me that her coworkers' most recent target was a new employee called "Chloe." The nursing-staff break room was buzzing with the scuttlebutt on Chloe's personal life and with how deficiently she was performing in her new job. And there was Natalie, feeling caught in the middle of the circle. She came to me for counsel.

Evil Listening

We've all been there, haven't we? We've all been in a conversation that suddenly takes a turn into gossip, and we're not sure what to do. We've learned that listening to gossip is almost as bad as speaking it. The Bible says, "A wicked man listens to evil lips; a liar pays attention to a malicious tongue" (Prov. 17:4). *The*

Message paraphrases that proverb, "Evil people relish malicious conversation; the ears of liars itch for dirty gossip." So there is another category of gossip in Scripture called *evil listening*.

Let me be clear. Not all listening is evil. The Bible commends and commands listening. The Word says, "Everyone should be *quick to listen*, slow to speak and slow to become angry" (James 1:19). Listening is important, and we are supposed to do it regularly. Sometimes we have to listen even to bad news about other people when those people are not present, especially if we are in a position of authority and responsibility.

But there is listening and then there is *listening*.

There is an evil kind of listening that receives gossip wickedly, and the difference, as we might expect by now, comes down to the heart. *How* we are listening is determined by *why* we are listening. The key is to listen in love. In Ephesians 5 we read, "Be imitators of God, therefore, as dearly loved children and live a life of love, just as Christ loved us and gave himself up for us as a fragrant offering and sacrifice to God" (Eph. 5:1–2). Our listening should be governed by Christlike love.

Light and Darkness

There will be times when we have to stand apart from those who are engaging in sinful gossip because it is not loving. Ephesians 5 calls us, as "children of light," not to partner with those who are still in the darkness (see 5:7–8).

> For you were once darkness, but now you are light in the Lord. Live as children of light. . . . Have nothing to do with the fruitless deeds of darkness, but rather expose them. For it is shameful even to mention what the disobedient do in secret. But everything exposed by the light becomes visible, for it is light that makes everything visible. (5:8, 11–14)

Not partnering with unbelievers doesn't mean not to be friends with them or not to spend time with them. It means not to take part in what they take part in if it is wicked. Even by just listening, we can find ourselves partnering with the darkness.

So, what do we do *instead*? What should Natalie do as a follower of Jesus at her job in the rehab center? Let's consider four biblical strategies for living as children of the light.

1. Pray and Weigh

I wish I could offer a simple formula for escaping gossip. When I started my research on this book, I was hoping to find a one-size-fits-all approach that could be automatically deployed. But life is messier than that, and God's wisdom is better than that too.

Some Bible teachers and authors give the impression that whenever gossip starts to flow, the only proper response is a hand-raised, palm-outward sanctimonious announcement: "Stop! This conversation is now gossip, and I will not be party to it," as if we, as Christians, are called to be the gossip police.

There surely is a time for confrontation, especially among fellow believers, but there are actually several biblical strategies that a believer can utilize to assist in these scenarios—not just one. In fact, it is important to consider the many factors at play in your particular situation:

- What, really, is going on here?
- What is my relationship to the person talking?
- What is my relationship to the person being talked about?
- How serious is this gossip?

- Is it a lie? Is it true? Is it just a rumor?
- What effects might this story have on others?
- Is this just a funny-ish thing someone did, or is it really shameful?
- Why is this story being told? What clues do I have for assessing the motives of the speaker?
- Is this the focus of the conversation, or are things going to just flow right on?
- Does this conversation fit the description of *bearing bad news behind someone's back out of a bad heart?*

The Spirit of Wisdom

When faced with gossip, we need wisdom and discernment to know how to respond. Thankfully, we are not alone in the world. Children of the light have the Holy Spirit living within them—"the Spirit of wisdom and revelation" (Eph. 1:17). The Spirit loves to give us the wisdom we need—we just need to ask Him for it. The Bible promises, "If any of you lacks wisdom, he should ask God, who gives generously to all without finding fault, and it will be given to him" (James 1:5). We need to dig for wisdom as well in the Bible (see Prov. 2:1–5). We can ransack our copies of the Scripture to guide us when we get into these gossip situations.

So my first piece of advice for Natalie was to *pray and weigh*.

Praying

When that conversation at work started to go down a darker path, she should shoot up a signal-flare prayer. *Pop! Whoosh!*

"Lord! Help! Help me to discern right now and to know what to do."

We should have an inner dialogue going on with the Lord all the time. The Bible tells us to "pray continually" (1 Thess. 5:17). This means that our hearts should be on speakerphone with our Lord. Dial Him up in the morning, and don't hang up all day. Especially in those times and situations when we think we might be getting into trouble, we need to get the Lord on the line right away. A simple "Father, help! Please give me Your wisdom" will do. The Lord loves to answer prayers like that. Often we don't have the wisdom we need because we don't even ask (see James 4:2).

Weighing

After we pray, and as we are listening for God's answer, we need to weigh carefully what we hear. Proverbs says, "The heart of the righteous weighs its answers, but the mouth of the wicked gushes evil" (15:28). This is one of those think-before-you-speak proverbs. The wicked person says whatever comes to his or her mind. The righteous person ponders, considers and weighs what he or she is about to say before saying it. As people talk to us, we need to weigh what's being said in our minds.

As we learned in chapter 4, we need to be careful not to fall into judging. Don't jump to conclusions. Get both sides. Consider the source. Suspend judgment. Weigh things out.

Many years ago I received a warning about a community member named "Aaron." I was told some pretty bad stories about Aaron, none of which have ever been officially confirmed. The person telling me these stories told me out of love for me and my family. He was not gossiping (although others have gossiped about Aaron to me at other times!). The person sharing these stories about Aaron was, as far as I could tell, trying to give me a biblical warning.

So I prayerfully weighed out what this person shared with me, and I decided to take the warning about Aaron to heart, even though I had nothing but stories to motivate my caution of him.

The Bible calls us to be discerning. Discerning the reality of a situation doesn't always take long. Often we don't have to pray or weigh for a long time in order to make a decision as to what is going on. In fact, most of the time we do it on the fly. I have a friend who gets anonymous phone calls in the middle of the night. On the other end of the line, there is always a voice telling her something bad about her husband. It doesn't take her a long time to weigh in on this. The only good thing for her to do in that situation is to hang up and maybe get a trace on the call to stop the harassment. Sometimes I get anonymous notes about people in our church listing things that those people have supposedly done or not done. I just tear them up. It does not always take long to weigh what is being said.

But if something we are told does begin to seem like gossip, then we have to take action and not just passively receive what's being told to us.

2. Avoid

Proverbs says, "A gossip betrays a confidence; so *avoid* a man who talks too much" (20:19). That's pretty straightforward. Don't go near a gossiper. Walk on the other side of the street. Get away from that person. You and I might need to skip out on some social situations if we know that all we will hear in them is sinful gossip. It might be a sacrifice, but it might also be worth it.

This proverb also applies to that gossip column, gossip television show, gossip blog, gossip magazine, gossip channel and gossip Facebook page. Those things are no good for our souls, and we need to avoid them like the plague. If you are addicted to them, get help, get accountability and start flushing them out of your system today.

But She's My Mother!

Sometimes we cannot avoid a person who gossips, simply because of our relationship to them. Natalie, for instance, cannot just avoid the nurses' break room and always eat on her own. Sometimes she needs to be there with the other staff.

In fact, like Natalie, we are often placed in these kinds of situations in order to influence people for Christ. We all know individuals who are part of social circles in which people easily fall into gossip. Yet as Christians, we are called to be salt and light, to strategically infiltrate those social circles. We don't become like the darkness, but we do love those who are not yet light.

In cases like these I think we need to avoid not the person but the topic. We need to redirect conversations, if we can, to avoid the gossip in them. I suggested to Natalie that when conversation turned to Chloe's faults, she should simply change the subject. "Natalie," I said, "ask the others about their plans for the weekend or about their family or about something you know that they love. Change the theme of the conversation."

That may sound a bit sneaky, but it is really just shepherding a conversation and acting as a leader. The Bible says, "Without wood a fire goes out; without gossip a quarrel dies down" (Prov. 26:20). Just removing the gossip can change the temperature in a room.

3. Cover

Proverbs says, "He who covers over an offense promotes love, but whoever repeats the matter separates close friends"

(17:9). The opposite of gossiping is "covering." Proverbs 10 also says, "Hatred stirs up dissension, but love covers over all wrongs" (10:12). What does it mean to "cover over wrongs"?

It does not mean to pretend something isn't happening or to sweep something under the rug. The Bible in no way gives perpetrators of crimes a blank check. Sin surely needs to be confronted. Proverbs is talking, however, about people who are uninvolved in the matter overlooking the offense. "Covering" means covering over a wrong, drawing a veil over it so that those who do not need to see it never do.

Covering Noah

After Noah came out of the ark in Genesis 9, he praised God and worshiped—then he grew a vineyard and got plastered. Genesis says, "He became drunk and lay uncovered inside his tent" (9:21). Scandal! Shame in the tent! Unfortunately, one of Noah's sons blabbed about it to his brothers. We do not know what he said, but my guess includes, "You'll never guess what our father has done. Come and see!" But the other two sons "took a garment and laid it across their shoulders; then they walked in backward and covered their father's nakedness. Their faces were turned the other way so that they would not see their father's nakedness" (9:23).

Would it have been wrong for Noah's sons to see their father in his folly? Maybe, maybe not. Regardless, two faithful sons went the extra mile to avoid seeing it, and they were clearly commended for doing so. They honored their father even when he was being dishonorable. They covered his offense.

We can do that for other people. Not in order to make an excuse for them but in order to cover over their shame so that their sin is not exposed to people, places or things it need not be.

One evening Heather Joy and I went out for dinner with some missionary friends, and our conversation turned to some mutual acquaintances who are also in pastoral ministry. Heather and I knew something bad about the other pastor couple that the missionary couple did not, and I really struggled to decide how much to say and how much to hold back. I like and trust the missionary couple, so it would have been easy for me to say too much. But I opted for sharing very little in an attempt to cover the other couple's disgrace. I was honest and forthright, but I did not share more than they needed to hear.

Bible teacher Joe Stowell says that we can do that from the get-go:

> Many times at social gatherings someone will get just far enough into a story to have everyone's attention and then say, "You know, I really shouldn't be telling you this." And of course the listeners all respond, "Oh, come on, you can't stop now. We won't tell." It would be refreshing to hear someone respond instead, "Good for you. Don't tell. I admire your self-control." We need to do what we can to stop negative talk before it gets spread.[1]

Good idea!

Sometimes it's as simple as using body language. We can say a lot with our nods and nudges and winks. Don't encourage gossip with your eyebrows.

Defending as Covering

I think this kind of covering includes defending someone's reputation, as well, especially if we know a story is false.

I was at a breakfast meeting once at which "Frank" shared a story about "Kevin" that was, as far as I knew, false. Frank said that Kevin had moved out on his wife and was living with another woman.

I said, "That's not true!" (Boy, was that was awkward to say!)

Unfortunately, it did turn out to be true, so I had to apologize to Frank, but I am still glad that I said what I did. It is right to defend someone's reputation. When I apologized to Frank, he said, "You were right to say something, Pastor Matt. I didn't need to be talking about Kevin anyway."

Sometimes the right thing to do is to say, "I'm not sure about that, but I don't think that it is any of our business." That's a loving rebuke, and it is covering over wrongs.

Natalie's Plan

Natalie and I brainstormed some more covering kinds of strategies for her workplace. She came up with the idea of offering an alternative interpretation to the gossip about Chloe. "Well, maybe she hasn't been trained very well yet on her new duties. I remember when I was just starting out and how hard it was to get the knack of it all," she determined to say.

Natalie decided to offer mercy to Chloe, even though she wasn't her friend yet and even though Chloe might not ever know that Natalie had said it. Isn't that great? Natalie was planning to not only resist gossip but to actively love in the midst of it!

We also came up with the idea of suggesting ways that the group of nurses who are prone to gossip could *help* Chloe get adjusted to her new job. That took it to another level—leading others in love.

Will Natalie's plan work? Maybe. I do know that it will please her Lord.

4. Go

Sometimes the best thing to do is to go directly to the one being talked about. Author Diana Kleyn shares a story about this in her book *Bearing Fruit: Stories about Godliness for Children*:

> There was once a minister's wife who had a very effective way of stopping a person from slander or gossip in her presence. Whenever someone would say something unpleasant about someone else, she would get her hat and coat.
>
> "Where are you going?" the person would ask.
>
> "I'm going to visit the person you mentioned and ask if what you said was true."
>
> People became very cautious about speaking unkindly about anyone in her presence.[2]

I'll bet they did!

If you hear a story about someone, do not just receive it. If you think you need to know whether or not the story is true, go directly to that person. This is even more important if the person has sinned against you. Our Lord says, "If your brother sins against you, *go* and show him his fault, just between the two of you. If he listens to you, you have won your brother over" (Matt. 18:15).

Go Together

If someone starts complaining to you about someone else, it is good to ask the complainer if he or she has talked about the problem directly with the subject of his or her complaint. You can say, "Have you talked with her about this? I am willing to go with you to help and to witness, but I don't think I should listen to any more until we've gone together to her." This can get messy, and it's not always fun. In a world that is still covered with darkness, light and darkness will tussle. But it is definitely worth it.

A friend of mine, "Ian," is an associate pastor in the Midwest. Soon after starting his new role, Ian heard two strong leaders in the church speak very negatively about the lead pastor. He immediately confronted these two and challenged them to go with him to the lead pastor to talk it out.

Ian said, "While I wondered if this would cost me, I can say two years later that one of those men is [now] a supportive leader who demonstrated humility and a willingness to speak directly and honestly to our lead pastor when he had disagreements [with him]. The other leader is not as supportive but is 'under control.'"[3] It wasn't easy, but Ian's willingness to go with these men dynamically changed the situation.

Go Alone

Sometimes the other person will not go with you. So in some cases, because it is loving to tell a person that others are gossiping about him or her, you'll need to go alone. Do this as carefully as you can. Try not to gossip about the person who has been gossiping! Be aware of your heart, and keep an eye on your motivations. Use the strategies we've learned in the previous chapters. Give as much of a sympathetic context for the comments as possible, and be gracious. But if a person's reputation is being significantly harmed, it is loving to let the target know what you have heard and then to pray with them that the situation can be straightened out.

Looking Ahead

Do you, like Natalie, now have a good idea of what you are going to do the next time you are faced with gossip? How can you act as a child of the light in a world still full of darkness?

In part 3 we are going to turn the tables. What if *you* or *I* are the ones being gossiped about? How do we respond to gossip that is spoken against us?

Questions for Group Discussion

1. Can you relate to Natalie's story? In what social settings are you regularly tempted to participate in gossip? What makes these circumstances difficult for you? What is your "go-to" strategy when others start gossiping around you? How do you normally react when others start gossiping around you?

2. Read Proverbs 17:4, Ephesians 5:1–17 and James 1:19. What is evil listening? How do you know if you are partnering with darkness?

3. The first alternative strategy in this chapter is to "pray and weigh." What does that mean to you? How do *you* do it?

4. Read the following scriptures, and discuss what the remaining three strategies—avoid, cover and go—mean (and do not mean). How have you seen wise people practice these strategies? What are common pitfalls when attempting to do them?

    a. Avoid: Proverbs 20:19

    b. Cover: Proverbs 10:12, 17:9

    c. Go: Matthew 18:15

5. Natalie was proactive and creative in making a plan to combat gossip. Why does love require so much thought and effort? What is *your* plan for the next time you are faced with gossip?

PART 3

RESPONDING TO GOSSIP

*Rescue me, O L*ORD*, from evil men; protect me from men of violence, who devise evil plans in their hearts and stir up war every day. They make their tongues as sharp as a serpent's; the poison of vipers is on their lips.*

Psalm 140:1–3

7

Responding in Faith

You will be gossiped about. If it has not happened yet, get ready, because someday you will find yourself in the crosshairs of the sin of gossip. My friend "William" did.

William is a Christian who owns rental property and tries to be just and merciful in managing it. But he had one tenant, "Nicholas," who refused to pay his rent on time and who let the balance of unpaid debt pile up. Nicholas also claimed to be a Christian, but instead of apologizing for his debt and paying up, he went through the community attacking William's character. Word slowly trickled back to William of what Nicholas had been saying about him to business owners, neighbors and friends. It hurt William a lot.

What would you do if you were in William's shoes? Are you ready to respond to gossip *when you are its target*?

Sadly, most of the time you will not know that you are a target of someone's harmful words. Perniciously, gossip is done behind our backs, when we are not looking, when we are not listening and when we are not present. So what do you do if, like William, you get wind of what is being said about you?

Before we can learn how to relate to the other people who have become involved in these situations, especially the ones who have perpetrated the wrong against us, we need to start with how we can relate *to God* when we find ourselves the target of gossip.

Songs of Experience

The Psalms are the richest quarry to mine in the Bible for learning how to righteously survive being the victim of other people's sins. The Psalms are songs of experience; the one we are about to read relates the experience of being attacked, chased, hated, slandered and of just about every other way of being sinned against! King David, especially, lived most of his life under attack, and his prayers, provided to us as songs in Scripture ,give us patterns to practice in our own lives today.[1]

Psalm 140 is one of David's songs of experience. In it David sings about a time when he lived as a target of gossip. As you read it, take careful note of *how* he talks to God:

> Rescue me, O LORD, from evil men; protect me from men of violence, who devise evil plans in their hearts and stir up war every day. They make their tongues as sharp as a serpent's; the poison of vipers is on their lips. "Selah"
>
> Keep me, O LORD, from the hands of the wicked; protect me from men of violence who plan to trip my feet. Proud men have hidden a snare for me; they have spread out the cords of their net and have set traps for me along my path. "Selah"
>
> O LORD, I say to you, "You are my God." Hear, O LORD, my cry for mercy. O Sovereign LORD, my strong deliverer, who shields my head in the day of battle—do not grant the wicked their desires, O LORD; do not let their plans succeed, or they will become proud. "Selah"

Let the heads of those who surround me be covered with the trouble their lips have caused. Let burning coals fall upon them; may they be thrown into the fire, into miry pits, never to rise. Let slanderers not be established in the land; may disaster hunt down men of violence.

I know that the LORD secures justice for the poor and upholds the cause of the needy. Surely the righteous will praise your name and the upright will live before you. (140:1–13)

Why Gossip Hurts

Before we unpack Psalm 140, we should think a little more about why being gossiped about is bad. What makes it so hard and so painful? It is a unique form of suffering, to be sure.

First, gossip is *betrayal.* It is a form of treason. A close friend, someone we trust, turns out to be the one bearing the bad news behind our back. King David experienced this kind of betrayal. In Psalm 55 he said,

> If an enemy were insulting me, I could endure it; if a foe were raising himself against me, I could hide from him. But it is you, a man like myself, my companion, my close friend, with whom I once enjoyed sweet fellowship as we walked with the throng at the house of God. (55:12–14)

William felt this way about Nicholas. He had been so glad to have a Christian tenant. What sweet fellowship they would enjoy! But Nicholas had stabbed him in the back.

Next, while betrayal always hurts, it can also leave us feeling vulnerable. It's easy to become fearful when we do not know what is being said about us. At one time we may have thought that all was well, but then we find out that there is an unseen buzz going on around us, and we cannot control it.

Are you feeling that right now? If you have recently found out that you are the target of gossip, you might be feeling helpless and out of control. To not know what is being said about us, much less to be able to control it, is scary.

In Psalm 55 David sings about that:

> My heart is in anguish within me; the terrors of death assail me. Fear and trembling have beset me; horror has overwhelmed me. I said, "Oh, that I had the wings of a dove! I would fly away and be at rest—I would flee far away and stay in the desert; . . . I would hurry to my place of shelter, far from the tempest and storm." (55:4–8)

David is saying that if he could have run away and hid, he would have. And *he was the king*! How much more can you and I feel scared and intimidated by sinful gossip?

Perhaps the most painful aspect of being gossiped about is the feeling of loss at the theft of our reputation. Let me ask you a trick question: is it good to care about our reputation? (Remember, that's a *trick* question. Don't answer too quickly!) Is it good to value your good name?

The answer is yes.

Proverbs 22 says, "A good name is more desirable than great riches; to be esteemed is better than silver or gold" (22:1). A good reputation is a blessed and valuable thing. A good name is something we should want and something we ought to cultivate, as much as it is in our control to do so. We should cultivate our reputations not through marketing, public relations or manipulating people's opinions of us but by being a man or woman of good character. Proverbs links a good name to wisdom. A wise man or woman will earn a good reputation.

But gossip often robs our reputations. Shakespeare captured that thought in his play Othello:

> Good name in man and woman, dear my lord,
> Is the immediate jewel of their souls [sounds like Proverbs 22:1!]:
> Who steals my purse steals trash; 'tis something, nothing;
> 'Twas mine, 'tis his, and has been slave to thousands;
> But he that filches from me my good name
> Robs me of that which not enriches him
> And makes me poor indeed.[2]

That's how my friend William felt. His reputation as a landlord was very important to him, and it seemed to be slipping out of his hands. So what do we do when we find ourselves lamenting the loss of our good name? Let's go back to Psalm 140.

1. Take It to the Lord

Notice where David goes when he gets into trouble. He says, "Rescue me, O LORD, from evil men; protect me from men of violence, who devise evil plans in their hearts and stir up war every day" (140:1–2). David takes his situation to the Lord first and foremost, and we should as well.

We don't tend to go to the Lord first though, do we? We take things into our own hands. We turn around and gossip about our enemies! We complain about those who are complaining about us. And we run around attempting to set the record straight.

William tried the record-straightening strategy first. He stopped by every place where Nicholas had spread gossip and attempted to talk with every single person Nicholas had poisoned against him. He said, "At first, I admit it was very difficult, since I came from a background of wanting always to vindicate myself. Not to get even but to be sure that everyone knew my side of the story."[3] But trying to reach everyone was impossible for him to do:

> It became evident that the task was overwhelming and was affecting my mental health. Relief came when I surrendered [Nicholas] to the Lord and myself as well. I had to take a hands-off approach and let the Lord defend my character. It was not about me but rather about what the Lord was doing in me. The burden lifted.[4]

When William finally took it to the Lord, he found freedom and joy, which he's still experiencing years later.

Tell It Like It Is

Notice how David cried out to the Lord in the beginning of Psalm 140. His requests were specific: "Rescue me! Protect me!" He talks to God about how his situation feels, and he does not mince words. "They make their tongues as sharp as a serpent's; the poison of vipers is on their lips" (140:3), David goes on to say. In other words, "Lord, these gossipers talk like snakes! They bite. Their words are full of poison. They speak Satan's language. Help!"

Do not be afraid to tell God how it is. God is not looking for us to just grin and bear things stoically, without feeling. Not at all! God invites us to tell Him exactly how we feel:

"Lord, I feel attacked."
"Lord, I feel betrayed."
"Lord, I feel scared."
"Lord, I feel angry."
"Lord, I hate being gossiped about!"
"Lord, take it away!"

Verse four of Psalm 140 says, "Keep me, O Lord, from the hands of the wicked; protect me from men of violence who plan to trip my feet" (140:4). David probably had it worse than you or I ever will. He had enemies who truly wanted him dead. Most of those who gossip about you and me don't actually want us to be killed, but the principle for us is the same as it was for David: take it to the Lord.

David continues his plea: "Proud men have hidden a snare for me; they have spread out the cords of their net and have set traps for me along my path" (140:5). He's essentially saying, "This is not easy, Lord! I don't like it. I'm going to trip. I'm going to fall."

Faith does not minimize our suffering. Faith does not say, "It's no big deal." Faith does not pretend that a situation is not painful or scary. What faith does do is take our problem to the One who really cares and can do something about it.

Remember to Whom You Are Talking

David's prayers were based on his relationship with God. As he continues his prayer, he says, "O Lord, I say to you, 'You are my God.' Hear, O Lord, my cry for mercy. O Sovereign Lord, my strong deliverer, who shields my head in the day of battle— do not grant the wicked their desires, O Lord; do not let their plans succeed" (140:6–8). David was not just asking some-god-out-there to do something for him. He was asking *his* God, the God with whom he was in covenant, the God to whom he belonged. David had already seen God work on his behalf. He is saying, "You have been there for me before, Lord, my strong deliverer. You have shielded my head in the day of battle. I know that You will be there again."

I do not know all the times that people have gossiped about

me. I can guess that there have been many of them. I am a semi-public figure in our little community and have been connected to various conflicts between people in my fifteen years of pastoral ministry. I surely deserve some of the gossip shared about me. Not that people *should* have shared bad news about me, but the truth is, some of the bad news was true. I am a sinner, and I have failed.

But throughout all the gossip that I *know* has been shared about me—and some of it has been deeply painful—God has protected me, my reputation and my ministry over and over again. I am profoundly thankful for that, and it helps me to be ready to take my challenges to the Lord *next* time. God has always shielded my head in the day of battle, so why wouldn't I turn to Him every time?

2. Ask God for Justice

David asked God to thwart the plans of the wicked. In fact, he asked for a *reversal*—that the bad things his enemies wanted for David would come back on their heads. David wanted justice:

> Do not grant the wicked their desires, O LORD; do not let their plans succeed, or they will become proud. "Selah"
> Let the heads of those who surround me be covered with the trouble their lips have caused. Let burning coals fall upon them; may they be thrown into the fire, into miry pits, never to rise. Let slanderers not be established in the land; may disaster hunt down men of violence. (140:8–11)

David and the other psalmists asked for justice again and again. They even asked that their reputations be protected. "Protect my reputation" is not a bad prayer. For example, Psalm 71 says, "In you, O LORD, I have taken refuge; let me never be put to shame" (71:1). That means, in effect, "Let me not look bad in the eyes of others. Protect my reputation. Not, ultimately, for myself but for You, Lord. But do not let my reputation be unjustly bad. Bring justice, O Lord!"[5]

Have you prayed for justice in your situation? If someone has gossiped about you and everyone seems to believe what that person has said, take the problem to the Lord, and ask Him for justice.

Two Difficult Things at the Same Time

You may, at first, have a hard time reconciling the psalmists' cries for justice with our Lord teaching us to love our enemies. You may not yet be able to pray Psalm 140:10—"Let burning coals fall upon them; may they be thrown into the fire, into miry pits, never to rise"—without bitterness and personal hate. It may even seem impossible for you to pray like that while at the same time holding out mercy for those who would repent. It is possible, however.

It takes becoming like Jesus, who is uniquely able to do two difficult things at the same time. I believe that if David's snake-tongued enemies had turned around and genuinely asked for forgiveness, David would have granted it gladly. David was famous for flashing hot with anger but also for dispensing grace. In that he was like his gracious Lord.

But the Lord is not just gracious. He is also holy and just, which means retribution for the unrepentant. God is both/and, not either/or.

So ask for justice while still loving your enemies. Jesus did that and made it possible for us to do it too through His work on the cross. His sacrifice satisfied the demands of justice while simultaneously dispensing mercy.

If the person who gossiped about you comes and asks for your forgiveness, give it. Quickly. Freely. Joyfully. Justice will still be done. Justice will always be done. So do not be afraid to forgive, and do not be afraid to humbly ask God to bring justice to your cause.

3. Believe that God Will Answer

In the last line of Psalm 140, David sings in confident faith, "I know that the Lord secures justice for the poor and upholds the cause of the needy. Surely the righteous will praise your name and the upright will live before you" (140:12–13). David *knew* that God would answer his requests. He *knew* things would work out rightly. He *knew* God would bring justice.

Consistently, the message of the Psalms is this: "Cast your cares on the Lord and he will sustain you; he will never let the righteous fall" (55:22). God will settle the score. God will see that justice is done for those who cry out for it. Your reputation will be saved! *But you may have to wait for it to happen.*

We live in an instant society in which we expect things to happen *now*, on our timetable. One of my favorite corny jokes says that scientists have invented a microwave fireplace—Americans can now have a relaxing evening in front of the fire in only eight minutes. Just as in other areas of our lives, we want our justice served right away.

But God's timetable and ours are not the same. One of my pastor friends likes to say, "God is seldom early but never late." Similarly, in Psalm 37, David says,

> Be still before the Lord and wait patiently for him; do not fret when men succeed in their ways, when they carry out their wicked schemes.
>
> Refrain from anger and turn from wrath; do not fret—it

leads only to evil. For evil men will be cut off, but those who hope in the LORD will inherit the land.

A little while, and the wicked will be no more; though you look for them, they will not be found. But the meek will inherit the land and enjoy great peace. (37:7–11)

You might have to wait a little while, but you can trust God to bring justice. You can trust God with your reputation.

Good, not God

Remember our trick question?

Is it good to care about your reputation?

Well, here's another answer to the question: "No. Not very much."

A good reputation is valuable, but it is not worth worrying about. Again, Psalm 37 says, "Do not fret [about it]—it leads only to evil" (37:8). Worrying about our reputation can take something good and make it a god, an idol. And idols are cruel taskmasters. They demand much and deliver little. William's worry about his good name troubled his sleep and messed with his health until he put it all in the Lord's hands. That's the kind of thing that happens when we start following idols—they always disappoint. Don't let yourself care too much about your reputation.

The Lord Secures Justice

The time it takes before God comes to our defense may feel longer than we can bear. For the Lord Jesus it was *after He died in injustice* that God made things all right again. Jesus was vindicated by His resurrection (see 1 Tim 3:16). For you and me it just might get worse before it gets better. But know this: it *will* get better! God has promised justice, and it is His very character to bring justice—to restore reputations and make everything right.

Jesus understands what we go through when we are gossiped about. If David understood what it meant to be under attack, how much more did Jesus, the One who is the fulfillment of the Psalms? Psalm 140 ends powerfully: "Surely the righteous will praise your name and the upright will live before you" (140:13). Jesus is living out verse 13 right now, and so are we—when we put our faith in the Lord.

Questions for Group Discussion

1. Tell the group about a time when you were the target of gossip. (Remember to be careful with other people's reputations as you tell the story.) How did it feel? How did you respond?
2. Read Psalm 140. What do you notice about David's relationship with the Lord? What did David ask for? What did David expect God to do? How did David talk to God?
3. How did you initially answer the trick question, "Is it good to care about your reputation?" Why?
4. William, the landlord, eventually had to surrender Nicholas, himself and his whole situation to the Lord. How do you think he went about doing that? What actions might he have taken? Do you think surrendering was something he did just once or that it was something he had to do repeatedly?

5. Perhaps the hardest part of trusting God with our reputation is waiting for God's justice to come. Does it help you to think of Jesus' delayed vindication? How?

Love your enemies and pray for those who persecute you.
Matthew 5:44

8

Responding in Love

Pastor "Sam" lost his job because of gossip. A disaffected woman in the California church Sam had pastored started complaining about him to her small group and later, to the church elders. She did not like some of the things Sam said from the pulpit nor how he came across personally. Some wise people suggested that she take her concerns directly to Pastor Sam, but she refused and kept on talking about him to others. Soon a negative opinion about Sam spread like gangrene throughout the church, despite nothing being said openly.

Instead of pushing for reconciliation, the elder board listened to the gossip. They decided to force Sam to resign. When it became obvious to Pastor Sam that he would not get to face his accuser and that he had no support from the leadership, he left the church quietly, confused and hurting.

What impressed me most, as Sam's friend watching this sad situation unfold from a distance, was how Sam acted in the face of gossip. Pastor Sam trusted God with his reputation. And, even more, Pastor Sam loved his enemies. Though hurt by the betrayals, he never lashed back at his opponents. He never took the gossiping route himself. He continued (and continues today) to seek reconciliation. He prayed for the church. He responded in kindness and grace. He acted like Jesus.

Love My *What*?!

What do you do with an enemy?

When someone gossips about you, he or she is acting as your enemy. That person may not be your enemy in any official way. He or she may, in fact, be your closest friend. But at the moment when bad news is being spread behind your back out of a bad heart, the person doing the spreading is acting as your enemy.

So again, I ask, what do you do with an enemy? Our Lord Jesus has the answer:

> You have heard that it was said, "Love your neighbor and hate your enemy." But I tell you: Love your enemies and pray for those who persecute you, that you may be sons of your Father in heaven. He causes his sun to rise on the evil and the good, and sends rain on the righteous and the unrighteous. If you love those who love you, what reward will you get? Are not even the tax collectors doing that? And if you greet only your brothers, what are you doing more than others? Do not even pagans do that? (Matt. 5:43–47)

In what we call His Sermon on the Mount (see Matt. 5–7), Jesus teaches us to love our enemies. In this particular section of the sermon, the Lord had been masterfully correcting misunderstandings and perversions of the law of God and setting forth both a correct interpretation of the law and His own divinely authoritative statements, that is, the law of Christ. Verse 43 notes the sixth time in this sermon that Jesus said, "You have heard that it was said," and the Lord countered this saying each time with something very different from what the people had heard before. What Jesus countered with is extremely different from what we hear now in our culture as well, not to mention from what other religions say and even from what our instincts might lead us to believe and do. Especially this one: love your enemies.

That certainly does not come naturally to us!

Leviticus does say, "Love your neighbor as yourself" (19:18). But the teachers of Jesus' day assumed that it meant, "Love your countryman, your brethren, your tribesmen." They believed that the corollary must be to "hate your enemy." But the law never says, "Hate your enemy." So Jesus counters, "But I tell you: Love your enemies and pray for those who persecute you" (Matt. 5:44).

Loving someone does not mean that we have to like them. Think about the last person whom you know gossiped about you. Do you have that person in your mind's eye?

Jesus is calling you to love that individual. Not love as in some touchy-feely-warm-and-fuzzy kind of thing. Not affection. But love as in an actively-seeking-someone's-good kind of thing. Love is an action, primarily, not a feeling. It seeks the good of another. It involves the heart but does not equate to liking someone or approving of what they do. Let's see just how active love is:

> Love is patient, love is kind. It does not envy, it does not boast, it is not proud. It is not rude, it is not self-seeking, it is not easily angered, it keeps no record of wrongs. Love does not delight in evil but rejoices with the truth. It always protects, always trusts, always hopes, always perseveres. Love never fails. (1 Cor. 13:4–8)

We are to show active love not just toward our friends but also toward our enemies.

Just Like Dad

When we love actively, we show our family resemblance. Jesus said, "Love your enemies and pray for those who persecute you, *that you may be sons of your Father in heaven*" (Matt. 5:44–45).

We know from what Jesus says elsewhere that we cannot become a son of God by being good. We cannot earn our way into sonship. We can, however, grow into our sonship by acting more and more in line with our new relationship with God and demonstrating that we are His children.

I look like my earthly father. His face and mine look very similar, and we're both bald. Hey, don't laugh! Bald is beautiful. My dad and I like to say that God only made a few perfect heads, and on the rest he put hair. Anyway, I'm glad I look like Dad, because it shows people that we are specially related to one another. Likewise, when Jesus tells us to love our enemies and we obey Him, we show the world that we are like our heavenly Dad. God sends sun and rain not just on His friends but on His enemies. He is kind and gracious to all. Even the evil tax collectors of Jesus' day and the organized crime bosses and drug dealers of our day love those who love them and greet those who greet them. There's nothing special or Godlike about that. But loving your enemies—that's something entirely different.

Different Strokes for Different Folks

Loving an enemy looks different in each situation. As I said before about resisting gossip, there is no one formula or three-step plan that works in every situation. Your response depends upon a lot of factors. For example, what kind of gossip did someone speak about you? Sure, all gossip is sinful, but there is a big difference between some idle chat about you shared by people you do not know and a malicious betrayal by a best friend. You will handle each case differently.

A few weeks ago my friend "Brooke" informed me that "Julia" had been gossiping about me to her and to others. Apparently, Julia felt scandalized by advice that I had given to a mutual acquaintance of ours. Brooke, in love, told me about Julia's actions, following the counsel we learned about in chapter 6 to go to the person being talked about. Truthfully, I don't even know Julia personally. She is a woman in our community whom I'm not sure I could point out in a lineup. I thanked Brooke for the information, but it hardly changed a thing regarding the way in which I related to Julia. I might be a little more aware of Julia and wary of her than I had been before, but that's okay. The Bible tells us to be wary of our enemies. Yet we're still supposed to love them.

Each situation we come across will call for discernment, prayer and sometimes wise counsel from other Christians. Pastor Sam needed to love his former church one way. I needed to love Julia another way. But hate is *never* an option.

So what, practically speaking, are our options? Here are four biblical love-in-action responses we can use when we find ourselves the target of gossip.

1. Pray

Again, Jesus said, "Love your enemies and pray for those who persecute you" (Matt. 5:44). That is easy to say but difficult to do. When someone hurts us, it is hard for us to ask God to help that person. It is one thing if the individual talked about us behind our back and then wised up and came to us for forgiveness. But if we find out about the gossip some other way, loving prayers might stick in our craw.

If you are having trouble praying for your enemies, think about Jesus. Think about His prayers for Judas and for those who tortured and killed Him on the cross. Meditate on Jesus' prayers for you and me before we were reconciled to Him. When we were still His enemies, Jesus prayed, "Father, I want those [not yet my children] to be with me where I am, and to see my glory, the glory you have given me" (John 17:24). Amazing! Jesus provides us with a perfect example of loving our enemies.

What should we pray for exactly? Pray for justice, as we saw to do in the last chapter. Pray even that our gossiping enemy's evil plans will backfire. But also pray for conviction and repentance and eventual blessing for our enemy. Sometimes if we pray for someone before confronting him or her, we'll find the person humbled and ashamed of his or her behavior and possibly willing to seek reconciliation. We'll find that God has already been working on that person's heart.

Pray also for yourself. Pray that you will have wisdom to know how to relate to the person who has hurt you so deeply. I suggest Paul's prayer in Philippians 1 as a great model to follow in asking God for smart love:

> And this is my prayer: that your love may abound more and more in knowledge and depth of insight, so that you may be able to discern what is best and may be pure and blameless until the day of Christ, filled with the fruit of righteousness that comes through Jesus Christ—to the glory and praise of God. (1:9–11)

2. Overlook

The Bible says, "A man's wisdom gives him patience; it is to his glory to overlook an offense" (Prov. 19:11). Ninety percent of the time, the right thing to do when we are the target of gossip is to simply overlook the offense.

Whether we should overlook an offense or not depends upon a number of factors including (1) what kind of gossip it is, (2) whether the story is true or false, (3) whether it is a secret you asked someone to keep but they shared it anyway and (4) the seriousness of the shared information. A great deal of gossip is just people sharing their bad opinions of us. In many of those cases, we can just overlook what they said and act as though the gossip did not happen. One of my friends says, "I'm glad when people gossip about me. At least they aren't talking about someone else!"

Overlooking is a kind of one-sided forgiving. It means that we just go on relating to the person in the same way we always did. That is what I did with Julia.

Overlooking does *not* minimize our pain. Gossip still hurts us. But overlooking an offense is a way to absorb the pain and to move on in love. I think it is cool that God has given us this glorious option for extending grace. Overlooking saves us a lot of time and trouble in our relationships and grows us into the patient image of God.

3. Confront

We cannot always overlook an offense. Love may call us to confront it, especially when the problem is between brothers and sisters in Christ. Jesus said, "If your brother sins against you, go and show him his fault, just between the two of you. If he listens to you, you have won your brother over" (Matt. 18:15). Notice that the first step is "just between the two of you." This is another reminder to us that we should not go behind a person's back and gossip about his sin against us to someone else! Further steps, if necessary, will include more people in a very wise and careful way (see Matt. 18:15–20).

Love doesn't just sweep things under the rug. Love goes to the person who is acting as an enemy and shows that person his or her fault so that relationship can be restored.

I mentioned in the introduction to this book a painful time in my pastoral ministry when harmful gossip about me was at its worst and I seriously thought about quitting the pastorate. There was one couple in particular who was spreading the bad news. When I found out about it, I approached them privately and confronted them in love. On the spot these people agreed that they had sinned, and they asked for my forgiveness! Our brotherhood was restored and even improved. We are better friends now than ever before.

Sometimes people will repent, and we can experience total forgiveness and reconciliation with them. At other times they will not repent, and we will need to be patient and to forebear with them. In those instances we need to release any bitterness we have, be ready to forgive them and continue toward reconciliation. Sadly, Pastor Sam is still longing for renewed fellowship with many of those who gossiped about him.

Questions Before Confronting

Keep a few questions in mind before you confront someone who has been gossiping about you.

Is it true? Maybe the person you want to confront should not be sharing certain information about you, but is the bad news a true story? Is there even a kernel of truth to it? Can you see why someone might have said it? Christians should look at more than one side of an issue. We need to be humble and to consider what part we may have played in a conflict.

If the bad news about you is not true, and it is something

shameful, then make sure that it does not become true. Make sure that you do not prove your critics right by the way you live. Peter said that Christ followers should keep "a clear conscience, so that those who speak maliciously [that's our word *katalaleo* again] against your good behavior in Christ may be ashamed of their slander" (1 Pet. 3:16). Do not live *their* story about you. Live the gossip down.

What can I learn from this? We can profit from just about any criticism we receive, even the ugly, behind-the-back kind. Just because our enemies are in the wrong does not mean that there isn't something we can learn from being talked about. God often provides good lessons for us that come from the unlikeliest of sources.

Pastors and other church leaders often miss this principle. We focus on the fact that someone is gossiping about us. "They are going about it all wrong," we say. Yet sometimes we need to listen to the message they are speaking, even if the medium is off kilter. Because of who we are in Christ, we have nothing to lose.

Of course, some backstabbing gossip is so malicious that the only thing we can learn from it is whom to beware. Here are a couple more questions to consider when planning to confront someone.

Should I defend myself? In the last chapter William wisely gave up trying to vindicate himself as a good landlord in the eyes of the people around town. Pastor Sam eventually did the same thing at his former church.

There are times, however, when you should defend yourself and your reputation. In the book of Acts and in the New Testament letters, Peter and Paul sometimes defended their actions and sometimes did not. Often it depended on what they thought they'd gain *for others* by trying. Ask yourself, *Would de-*

fending myself in this situation be loving? Then the Lord will direct your steps as you trust in Him.

Can I rejoice in this? If the gossip is untrue and it has come about because we are following the Lord Jesus, then God says that we should actually rejoice!

When I thanked Pastor Sam for telling me his story and showing the way through gossip with godly honor, he said,

> Jesus taught us that we're blessed when we're wrongly accused (which must involve being gossiped about), and so I have learned and am still learning much from this God-ordained experience. I praise our Triune God for letting me taste a small bite of betrayal for Christ's sake—that I may know Jesus more and be refined for His kingdom work.[1]

Pastor Sam has learned to follow his Lord's instruction: "Blessed are you when people insult you, persecute you and falsely say all kinds of evil against you because of me. Rejoice and be glad, because great is your reward in heaven, for in the same way they persecuted the prophets who were before you" (Matt. 5:11–12).

4. Repay Evil with Good

In essence, loving our enemies is returning good for evil. I believe that the apostle Peter was meditating on Jesus' teaching from Matthew 5 when he wrote First Peter 3. Peter was preparing his readers for persecution, believing that suffering would be the norm for Christians until Jesus returns. Peter wrote,

> Do not repay evil with evil or insult with insult, but with blessing, because to this you were called so that you may inherit a blessing. For, "Whoever would love life and see good days must keep his tongue from evil and his lips from deceit-

ful speech. He must turn from evil and do good; he must seek peace and pursue it. For the eyes of the Lord are on the righteous and his ears are attentive to their prayer, but the face of the Lord is against those who do evil." (3:9–12)

I don't know about you, but I want the eyes of the Lord on me and His ears attentive to my prayers! I surely don't want the face of the Lord to be against me. God's loving attention is focused on His people when we use our tongues righteously and when we seek good for others—especially for our enemies.

If people have gossiped about you, make sure that your basic stance is *for them*. This doesn't mean that you must trust them in the same way you did before they gossiped about you. It does mean you should want what is best for them, even at a personal cost. That is how Jesus loved us, isn't it? While we were still His enemies, Christ died for us (see Rom. 5:8).

Returning blessings for beatings seems crazy to the world, but that's what we do as Christians. Paul's personal testimony was, "We are fools for Christ. . . . When we are cursed, we bless; when we are persecuted, we endure it; when we are slandered, we answer kindly" (1 Cor. 4:10, 12–13). In other words, we bear the family resemblance, living like Christ did. And when we do that, Christ says we will be rewarded.

Great Reward

Jesus asked, "If you love those who love you, what reward will you get?" (Matt. 5:46).

Answer: "None."

But the opposite is true. If you *love* your enemies, you will be richly rewarded. If you love the person who gossips about you, then God will pay you back. That is the blessing that Peter said we would inherit (see 1 Pet. 3:9). In a parallel passage Jesus promised, "Love your enemies, do good to them, and lend to them without expecting to get anything back. Then *your reward will be great*, and you will be sons of the Most High" (Luke 6:35). Sounds exciting to me!

Looking Ahead

Of course, it still does not make all this easy. Being gossiped about produces suffering. It is painful. Jesus knows that. He had it worse than anyone. Jesus never deserved any of the gossip about Him, and people called Him a bastard, a son of the devil and a partner with Satan. He knows how hard it is, but He loved His enemies. He calls us to love ours too.

There is only one chapter in part 4, but its message is for all of us. What do we do after giving in to the temptation to gossip? Is there any hope for us?

Questions for Group Discussion

1. Is it harder for you to trust God with your reputation or to love someone who gossips about you? Why do you think this is so?

2. Read Matthew 5:43–48, and discuss what you see. In what ways is Jesus' teaching different from what other people or our own instincts say? What does it mean (and not mean) to love your enemies?

3. Have you ever tried praying for your enemies? How did that go? Would you do it differently next time?

4. Read Proverbs 19:11 and Matthew 18:15–20. When should we overlook gossip, and when should we con-

front it? What principles do you use when you make a decision to do either? What questions do you keep in mind?

5. Read Luke 6:35 and First Peter 3:9–16. How does the promise of great reward factor into your choices to repay evil with good? Do you have an enemy whom God is calling you to love in a particular way this coming week?

PART 4

REGRETTING GOSSIP

If we confess our sins, He is faithful and just and will forgive us our sins and purify us from all unrighteousness.

1 John 1:9

9

Regretting Gossip

As much as we may want to, we can't just take words back. When we are guilty of bearing bad news behind someone's back out of a bad heart, we cannot retrieve the things we have said. The gossip is now out there. As author Lori Palatnik says, "Gossip is like a fired bullet. Once you hear the sound, you can't take it back."[1]

I see a great deal of shame on the faces of those who have given in to gossip. The choice morsels seemed so irresistible, so tantalizing, at the time of these people's transgression. Now they can't take back what they have said. The damage is done.

Intense Regret

Do you remember Lynette, the teacher you read about in chapter 2 who got sucked into the quicksand of gossip in the teachers' lounge? One of the things she said to me really stuck out: "As I type this, I remember how much I hated myself then and still hate myself now for doing and saying what I did."[2] Those are strong words. In her confession I hear shame, disgrace, condemnation and even self-loathing.

Why do we feel so bad when we have given in to gossip?

Gossip Is Sin

Our consciences are warning us that we have offended a holy God who *hates* gossip. Paul says in Romans 1, "The wrath [the hot anger] of God is being revealed from heaven against all the godlessness and wickedness of men who suppress the truth by their wickedness" (1:18). He goes on to list gossip as part of that wickedness: "They [sinners] are full of envy, murder, strife, deceit and malice. They are *gossips*, slanderers, God-haters, insolent, arrogant and boastful; they invent ways of doing evil; they disobey their parents; they are senseless, faithless, heartless, ruthless" (1:29–31). Finally he says, "Those who do such things deserve death" (1:32). If we give in to the temptation to gossip and have any conscience left, we are going to rightly feel some regret!

Gossip Hurts People

Deep down, we know we are hurting others when we gossip. An old axiom says that gossip hurts at least three people: the one being spoken about, the one hearing the gossip, and the one speaking it. That is true, but the most painful of those positions to be in at the time is to be the target of the gossip, especially if the story is just a rumor.

Proverbs 12:18 says, "Reckless words pierce like a sword, but the tongue of the wise brings healing." When I look back on the times when I have recklessly gossiped about others, one of the things I regret the most is how what I said hurt those people.

Gossip Is Irretrievable

On top of offending God and harming others, gossip is

something that we can't just take back. The toothpaste is out, and there is no way to stuff it back in the tube.

Rabbi Joseph Telushkin tells this story:

> In a small Eastern European town, a man went through the community slandering the rabbi. One day, feeling suddenly remorseful, he begged the rabbi for forgiveness and offered to undergo any penance to make amends. The rabbi told him to take a feather pillow from his house, cut it open, scatter the feathers to the wind, then return to see him. The man did as he was told, then came to the rabbi and asked, "Am I now forgiven?"
>
> "Almost," came the response. "You just have to do one more thing. Go and gather all the feathers."
>
> "But that's impossible," the man protested. "The wind has already scattered them."
>
> "Precisely," the rabbi answered. "And although you truly wish to correct the evil you have done, it is as impossible to repair the damage done by your words as it is to recover the feathers."[3]

So if we can't recover the feathers, what *can*, and *should*, we do?

1. Repent of Sinful Gossip

The apostle Paul was just about ready to make his third ministry trip to Corinth, but he was concerned about what he would find when he got there. The Corinthian church had been going steadily downhill:

> I am afraid that when I come I may not find you as I want you to be, and you may not find me as you want me to be. I fear that there may be quarreling, jealousy, outbursts of anger, factions, slander, *gossip*, arrogance and disorder. I am afraid

that when I come again my God will humble me before you, and I will be grieved over many who have sinned earlier and have not *repented* of the impurity, sexual sin and debauchery in which they have indulged. (2 Cor. 12:20–21)

Gossip was a major problem troubling Corinth, and Paul was concerned that the Corinthians may not have repented of it. Repentance is not just feeling bad about our sin. It is turning away from sin and turning toward the Lord. It is a turn in our heart that changes the direction of our lives. Repentance is also the only way forward after falling prey to sinful gossip.

True Confessions

The first step of repentance is to confess our sins. To confess means to completely agree with God about our sin. It is telling God that we have sinned by naming what we have done, owning it and agreeing that it was wrong and an offense against Him. The Bible promises, "If we confess our sins, [God] is faithful and just and will forgive us our sins and purify us from all unrighteousness" (1 John 1:9). What a tremendous promise!

True confession does not fall back on excuses like, "The devil made me do it!" "I didn't want to, but that woman made me gossip" or, "Lord, I feel bad about gossiping, but if You knew the circumstances, You'd have done it too."

These are not confessions. A confession says, "Lord, what I did was wrong. I should not have said that. I should not have listened to that. It was against Your law. It hurt someone. It deserves death. I was not glorifying You when I gossiped. I am sorry."

True confession certainly includes our emotions. We should feel bad about having been bad. But confession also includes agreeing with our whole heart that our gossiping was sin.

2. Retract the Sinful Gossip

You never know what people are going to say after a worship service. Like many pastors, I stand at the back door of the church shaking hands with people and greeting them as they leave. Some people like to talk about the sermon, while others chat about the weather or what is going on with their families. Sometimes they ask for prayer.

A few years ago a young man met me at the door after church and said, "Pastor, I need to ask your forgiveness. I've been gossiping about you." Boy, did that take me back a few steps! At first I didn't know what to say. I really appreciated his sincerity. Finally I said, "Of course, I forgive you."

"I want you to know that I am not only apologizing to you," the man continued, "but I am going to go back to the people I have gossiped to about you and seek their forgiveness for poisoning their minds against you." And he did. That took guts, and it was a true sign of repentance.

Discernment Required

Retracting gossip also takes wisdom and discernment. It is something for us to pray about and to ask the Holy Spirit's guidance on. At times we may need to seek out wise and godly counsel before running around apologizing to people.

There are times when retraction doesn't matter much at all. If we have been gossiping about a celebrity whose face is on the cover of today's *People* magazine, I don't think it's necessary to send her a letter of apology. (But knock it off anyway!)

Most of the time our apologies should reach as broadly as those who were affected by our gossip, but in some cases, it might make a relationship worse if you approach people and apologize for gossiping about them. For example, if you gossiped a negative opinion about one of your friend's choices to someone else, it might be best to just apologize to the person with whom you shared it, not to the one about whom you talked. If your friend did not know you thought something bad about her in the first place, it might not help to tell her now.

In many ways whether or not we go to every single person involved and apologize depends on the seriousness of what we did. Ask yourself the following:

- How serious was the content of my gossip?
- How seriously could the gossip affect my relationship with this person or impact his reputation?
- How far did the bad news travel?

After prayer and godly counsel, if you are not sure whether or not you should confess, I would advise you to err on the side of Jesus' Golden Rule. If your places were switched, would you want that person to come to you and retract the gossip?

From the Heart

The most important confession is to God. If we yawn and say, "Oh, that's not so hard! What is really hard is going to the person I was talking about," then we do not realize how devastatingly wicked our sin really is.

When King David finally repented of his sin with Bathsheba, he wrote a prayer song to the Lord that said, "Against you, you only, have I sinned and done what is evil in your sight" (Ps. 51:4). David did not mean that he had not sinned against Bathsheba, Uriah and all of Israel. He meant that all sin is first and foremost an offense against a holy God. The wrath of God is being revealed against those who gossip, so we must confess our sin to Him first.

Genuine repentance means confessing more than the words that we used to gossip, but also confessing the heart behind it. Remember, all talk is heart talk. Say, "Lord, I am sorry that I said those things about her. I was being ruled by a lust for power." Or, "Lord, my heart was full of hateful grumbling." Or, "Lord, I was afraid of the crowd and was not fearing You. Please forgive me." The most amazing thing is that *He does*.

3. Receive Jesus' Cleansing

We do not have to live in self-loathing, condemnation and regret. We can live as forgiven, cleansed and pure people. Our scripture says, "If we confess our sins, he is faithful and just and *will forgive us our sins and purify us from all unrighteousness*" (1 John 1:9).

Are you secretly worried that God will not really forgive you for your gossip (or for any of your sins, for that matter)? Are you afraid that maybe He will bring up your sin again and thrust it in your face? He won't. He is faithful to forgive. In fact, John says that He *must* do that. God has promised to forgive us if we confess our sins, and He always keeps His promises.

But even more than the fact that God is faithful to His promises, it would be *unjust* of God not to forgive. Sure, it seems as if it should be just for God to punish. And according to Scripture, it would! Romans 1:32 says, "Those who do such things [as gossip] deserve death [by God's righteous decree]." The just punishment for our sins is God's holy wrath, punishment and condemnation. Yet John says that God is "faithful and just" to forgive.

Why is forgiving our sins considered *just*?

Because of the cross. The cross is what makes it just for God to forgive us. Because our sins have already been paid for, it would be *unjust* for God to refuse forgiveness. John goes on to say,

> My dear children, I write this to you so that you will not sin [resist gossip!]. But if anybody does sin [and regrets it], we have one who speaks to the Father in our defense—Jesus Christ, the Righteous One. He is the atoning sacrifice for our sins, and not only for ours but also for the sins of whole world. (1 John 2:1–2)

Jesus Christ died for our sins. He bore the punishment that we deserved for gossiping. He became the atoning sacrifice, or propitiation for our sins, satisfying the wrath of God in our place. Jesus has now become our advocate.

This is why penance is not necessary. Penance, as it is popularly practiced, is taking on a penalty or a punishment to help atone for a sin. But our sin has already been paid for. When He was on the cross, Jesus announced, "It is finished" (John 19:30). And it is.

Only because of what Jesus did for us on the cross, God is "faithful and just and will forgive us our sins and purify us from all unrighteousness." Not because of any sincerity of ours. Not because of our righteousness but because of His.

That's Not How It Works

In my research on the subject of gossip, I read quite a few Jewish moral teachings against gossip. Much of what the Jews have said over the years has been very helpful, and we can learn from their reflections on the subject. But most of them do not believe in Jesus as the Messiah, so these Jews have a faulty understanding of grace and no understanding of the cross. They have to make up other things to substitute for it.

For example, in the book *Gossip: Ten Pathways to Eliminate It from Your Life and Transform Your Soul*, Jewish author Lori Palatnik and co-author Bob Burg teach that after we stop gossiping, regret what we've done and confess our sin to God, there is still one thing left to do. The authors say, "Once you have completed these steps [of repentance], God accepts your return, but it's still on the books, so to speak. Yes, it is noted that it was taken care of, but it's still there."[4]

Did you catch that? They go on,

> How do you completely edit it out? By going to the next step, called *teshuvah gamurah*, or "complete return." . . . This occurs after you have gone through the steps, time has passed, and God, sometimes with a very good sense of humor, puts you in the same position as when you originally made the mistake, and you do not repeat the mistake. When this occurs, not only are you forgiven, but it's as if you never made the original mistake. It is edited out of the story of your life, as if it had never happened.[5]

No. This is *not* how it works! We are not forgiven and cleansed because we eventually get it right and stop messing up. Christians are forgiven and cleansed only because of the death and resurrection of Jesus Christ.

> This righteousness from God comes through faith in Jesus Christ to all who believe. There is no difference, for all have sinned and fall short of the glory of God, and are justified freely by his grace through the redemption that came by Christ Jesus. God presented him as a sacrifice of atonement, through faith in his blood. (Rom. 3:22–25)

Romans chapter 1 tells us that we were found guilty, but Romans chapter 3 declares us not guilty because of the righteousness of Christ reckoned to our account.

No Feather-gathering Either

We are also not forgiven and cleansed because we ran around town finding each and every one of those feathers that we scattered! Rabbi Telushkin's story of the feather pillow is good for reminding us that our words have consequences that we cannot control. But our forgiveness is not tied to finding all the feathers and returning them to the pillowcase. Our forgiveness is tied to the precious blood of Jesus Christ, the atoning sacrifice for our sins.

Receive that cleansing.

Receive it for the first time or for the millionth. If you have never trusted Jesus Christ as your Savior, I invite you to do it now. Yes, your gossiping deserves death, but Jesus died so you would not have to die eternally. Repent right now and trust Jesus Christ as your Savior and Lord, and God will forgive you and purify you from all unrighteousness. He promises! You can be clean.

If you are already a follower of Jesus Christ and have messed up this week by giving in to gossip or some other sin worthy of death, do not wallow in self-hate. Turn to the Lord again for cleansing now. His blood is so powerful!

Repentance is much more powerful than regret. The gospel is much more powerful than gossip. We have seen how the gospel gives us power to resist gossip, but it also has the power to release forgiveness for us.

Hear this, Christian. *God knows where every single feather is and has the sovereign power to find each one and bring them home again.* The Bible says that God will work everything to His glory and for His people's good (see Rom. 8:28). That is how good the good news is. Receive Jesus' cleansing and walk in it.

Questions for Group Discussion

1. Tell the group about a time when you found gossip to be irresistible and then regretted your actions. What happened? How did you feel? How do you feel about it today?

2. Read First John 1:5–2:2 and then share your observations. What does it mean to truly confess our sins? What gets in the way of confession? What excuses have you tried to justify your gossip?

3. Have you ever gone to one of your victims and repented of your gossip about him or her? Why or why not? How did it go?

4. The world offers false gospels such as "Get it right the next time, and then you'll be forgiven." Why is that false gospel so attractive to us? What effect does believing it have on us?

5. The devil wants you to live in defeat, and he says to us, "You can't be completely forgiven, just as you can't gather up all those feathers." But Christians know better. How is the gospel greater than gossip? How can you hold your head up and walk in renewed victory?

6. Read Psalm 15. It portrays a picture of a godly person who lives an unshakeable life. What characterizes such a person? Pulling together everything you have learned throughout this study, what are key truths for you to keep in mind for becoming a Psalm 15 man or woman?

No longer will there be any curse.
Revelation 22:3

A Final Word:
The End of Gossip

Gossip seems overwhelming. The more I studied it, talked about it and wrote about it, the more it seemed inevitable and unstoppable. As I said in this book's introduction, "Gossip is everywhere." *What can a little book do about it?*

Trying to resist gossip feels like standing on the beach and talking the tide out of coming in. Not going to happen.

And yet isn't that what Christians do? Go against the tide? We are people whose lives flow in a different direction than the lives of those in the world (see Rom. 12:2). We swim against the current, knowing that there is coming a day when the glory of the Lord will cover the earth like the waters cover the sea—even when there is no sea, no chaotic, overpowering evil (see Hab. 2:14; Rev. 21:1).

No more being overwhelmed. No more gossip to be resisted.
There will no longer be any bad news!
Amen. Come, Lord Jesus.

BONUS CHAPTER

FOR CHURCH LEADERS

How good and pleasant it is when brothers live together in unity!
Psalm 133:1

Bonus Chapter for Church Leaders

Cultivating a Gossip-resistant Church

How good and pleasant it is when brothers live together in unity! It is like precious oil poured on the head, running down on the beard, running down on Aaron's beard, down upon the collar of his robes. It is as if the dew of Hermon were falling on Mount Zion. For there the LORD *bestows his blessing, even life forevermore.*

(Ps. 133)

What images come to your mind when you think of *unity among brothers*? For King David it was a gooey beard and a dew-drenched mountain. I'm sure those are not our typical pictures of brotherly love! But for David and the Israelite families singing Psalm 133 as they entered Jerusalem to celebrate the great Jewish feasts, there were few things better.

God loves unity among brothers. For the Israelites this was talking about literal brothers—kinsmen and clansmen. For us the church is a family of brothers and sisters in Christ knitted together in comm*unity* and oneness. At least, we should be. When we are unified, God says that it is "good and pleasant."

Good = Holy

I used to think that Psalm 133 was weird. What did these exotic images mean? What's up with Aaron's oily beard? After studying the psalm some more, however, I think Aaron's gooey beard is the perfect picture of the utter holiness of unity.

Precious oil is often a symbol in the Bible of the sanctifying work of the Holy Spirit. Anointing someone with oil consecrated him and symbolized his being set apart for a special purpose. In this case Aaron was anointed by Moses to become the high priest of Israel. (Read Exodus 29 and Leviticus 8 to get the full story.)

Psalm 133 tells us that this was a total consecration. We get the picture of this slick, fragrant, perfumey stuff sliding down Aaron's head, onto his beard and down onto the collar of his robes. Aaron was completely immersed in oily goo.

This may sound gross to our foreign and modern ears, but to the ancient Israelite there was nothing more sacred. The most consecrated person in their whole community was completely covered by a visible marker of holiness. David could not think of a more precious image to use as a comparison to the sacredness of unity. Unity among brothers is utterly holy.

Pleasant = Refreshing

The second strange (to us) image is the dew of Mount Hermon descending on Mount Zion. Mount Hermon is actually more than a mountain. It is a massive range that rises 9,200 feet above sea level and extends twenty miles from north to south. Mount Zion, on the other hand, is relatively small. Zion is more like a hill upon which the city of Jerusalem was built. It is only 2,500 feet above sea level.

Do you see the picture?

Imagine the dew of great *Hermon* being poured on little *Zion*! Imagine the deluge of water that would carry life-giving sustenance to a drier, more weary land. Imagine how green and fertile and rich and refreshed Zion would be if it were drenched in Hermon's dew. Another awesome analogy. Unity is completely refreshing!

Unity is like stepping into an air-conditioned home after being outside in the sweltering heat. It feels so invigorating, especially to a world like ours that is so fractured.

You might be asking, "Why all this stuff about beards and mountains in a chapter about cultivating a gossip-resistant church?" Quite frankly, we as leaders need to see how high the stakes are. This scripture illustrates a breathtaking vision of the beauty of unity, and it was critical for me to emphasize how much God values that quality among His people. The Lord celebrates unity with songs like Psalm 133! He calls it *blessing*: "For there [dew drenched Zion] the LORD bestows his blessing, even life forevermore" (133:3). Unity is *that* important.

Loose Lips Sink Fellowships

Because of His great love for the unity of His people, God *hates* anything that threatens unity the way gossip does:

> There are six things the LORD *hates*, seven that are detestable to him: haughty eyes, a lying tongue, hands that shed innocent blood, a heart that devises wicked schemes, feet that are quick to rush into evil, a false witness who pours out lies and *a man who stirs up dissension among brothers.* (Prov. 6:16–19)

God hates dissension. The Bible says that God hates those who sinfully divide His church. Of course, the Lord does not endorse unity at *any* cost. He loves truth and may require that we divide from others for the sake of important differences. There are times when it is necessary to divide, but God hates the *unnecessary* division of His people.

Sinful disunity is unholy and the complete opposite of refreshing. It drains, saps and sucks the life out of people. God hates sinful disunity among brothers, and few things create disunity like gossip. Proverbs says, "A perverse man stirs up dissension, and a gossip separates close friends" (16:28). Loose lips sink friendships and fellowships.

Know this: gossip can mean the end of a local church. It may start as a confidential prayer request about something that is none of anyone's business and grow into a full-fledged conflict that destroys an entire local fellowship.

Our Job: Gossip-proofing the Church

As noted earlier, Paul feared that division would happen at Corinth. He said, "I am afraid that when I come I may not find you as I want you to be, and you may not find me as you want me to be. I fear that there may be quarreling, jealousy, outbursts of anger, factions, slander, gossip, arrogance and disorder" (2 Cor. 12:20). That is why he wrote to the church.

Paul knew that it was *the leaders' job* to address gossip in the local church. As pastors, elders and every other kind of church leader, we need to value unity as the Lord does and do whatever is in our power to cultivate a gossip-resistant culture in our local fellowships.

How much of a problem is gossip in the church you serve? In the years I've been pastoring Lanse Free Church, we have enjoyed a high level of unity. Aside from the painful experiences I've recounted in previous chapters, Lanse Free has not been at all like Paul's experience at the "First Church of Corinth." We have enjoyed the holy and refreshing blessing of unity. As much as it depends on me, I want to keep it that way.

I hope your experience has been similar to mine, but many churches are plagued with festering gossip. What can we do about that as the leaders of God's flock? Here are ten biblical principles to keep in mind as we develop strategies to gossip-proof our local churches.

1. Pray Hard

Prayer is usually the first point on a list like this, but I really mean it. God cares more about the church than we do. He bought it with His own blood! The church is God's, not ours, so we need to take its needs to Him. Jesus prayed for our unity; how could we think that we could skip doing the same (see John 17:23)?

Pray against gossip. Pray that the flock you help to lead will resist the temptations of ungodly speech and pursue up-building speech instead. Pray for each of the next nine principles to be realized in your local fellowship. Paul says, "Pray in the Spirit on all occasions with all kinds of prayers and requests. With this in mind, be alert and always keep on praying for all the saints" (Eph. 6:18). By the way, when Paul says "all," he means "all." We have a tendency to stop praying for those with whom we are having trouble. We'd rather complain about them to other people. But God wants us to take our complaints to Him.

Lead the people of the church in prayer against gossip. Adopt Psalm 141 as a model for corporate prayer: "Set a guard over [our] mouth[s], O LORD; keep watch over the door of [our] lips. Let not [our] heart[s] be drawn to what is evil, to take part in wicked deeds with men who are evildoers; let [us] not eat of their delicacies" (141:3–4). The Holy Spirit is delighted to answer prayers like that!

2. Set a Godly Example

Leaders are to be thermostats, not thermometers. We do not just measure the spiritual temperature of our congregations; we help to set it by our examples. It is a scary thing to realize, but our people are listening to us all the time and will learn to talk the way we do. If we gossip, they will too. If we are careful with our tongues and are self-controlled, they will have a good model to follow.

Basic mastery of our mouth is one of the qualifications for church leaders in the Pastoral Letters. For example, an elder must be self-controlled (see 1 Tim. 3:2; Titus 1:8). A deacon must be sincere (see 1 Tim. 3:8). The Greek word translated as "sincere" in the NIV is actually "not *dilogous*," a word which may have been made up by Paul for this letter. It literally means "not talking twice," which could mean "not two-faced" or "not repeating a matter," that is, not a gossip.[1]

Women involved in leadership are warned against gossip as well. Paul writes, "Women *must* likewise *be* dignified, not malicious gossips, but temperate, faithful in all things" (1 Tim. 3:11, NASB) and, "Older women likewise are to be reverent in their behavior, not malicious gossips nor enslaved to much wine, teaching what is good" (Titus 2:3, NASB).

Take these qualifications for leaders seriously. If you do not already do this, improve your screening process for leaders by incorporating an evaluation of a candidate's character, including his or her habits of speech.

While writing this chapter, I received a call from a senior pastor whose outreach pastor's wife was unhappy with the way her husband was being treated by the church board. It was clear that this woman misunderstood several aspects of what the leaders had said and done in making recent decisions. Mrs. Outreach

Pastor was not pleased. She felt as if her husband was being mistreated. Sadly, instead of bringing her concerns directly to the leadership, she began to complain to her friends in small groups and in large group meetings. I encouraged the senior pastor to work with his leaders to address this with her and her husband *immediately*.

Setting a godly example starts with taking a good look at ourselves. I have become painfully aware of my own shortcomings in the area of gossip while writing this book. I have gone to others to make apologies and amends, and I have set new standards for myself. What kind of an example are you setting for the flock under your care?

3. Teach Against the Sin of Gossip

I wrote this book, in large part, because there were very few teaching resources available for the local church to learn how to counter gossip. Our culture encourages gossip. The church has been ignorant about it. We must do a better job of teaching our people how to recognize, resist and respond to gossip.

Plan a sermon series or a special class on the subject. Have your small groups read this book or *Stop the Runaway Conversation* by Michael Sedler. Do not assume that your people know what is right and what is wrong. Teach them.

Train them too. Give your people illustrations, examples and stories that tell them what kinds of things to say in place of gossip. Early in my ministry at Lanse Free, two prominent members left our church because of a conflict they had with each other and consequently with our leadership. At a church family meeting, I addressed this situation and took time to teach the membership how to respond. I passed around a handout with four points on it:

1. Keep loving them.
2. Love them enough to confront them.
3. Do not engage in gossip.
4. Most of all, pray.

I elaborated on each point and gave our people specific words that they could use in relating to the departing members. For point 3 I said,

> I am sure that there are many stories circulating about what is going on between [name] and [name]. Resist the temptation to listen to rumors and to pass on stories. Proverbs 26:20 says, "Without wood a fire goes out; without gossip a quarrel dies down." We as a church need to commit ourselves to not putting any fuel on this fire.

And by and large, we didn't! I am glad I taught on this early in my ministry. I also touch on it regularly, having preached a nine-message series on resisting gossip that ultimately became this book. From the feedback I have received, it seems that our church stands strong against gossip because I taught what the Bible says about it.

4. Encourage Loving Small Talk

While we teach against the sin of gossip, we also need to encourage the right kind of small talk. Remember, not all small talk is sinful. In fact, small talk can be a powerful force for good. David Powlison says,

> Small talk: it is either a way for me to say, "I don't want to know you and I don't want you to know [me] and so I am going to keep it light and make it as quick as possible and see

you later." Or small talk is a way to say, "I care about you. I would like to get to know you." We can talk about a football team or the weather and it is actually an expression of two human beings making that connection, but it is because we love each other or want to know each other. Small talk is going to be judged by God for the kind of deep intentionality it is.[2]

This is wise. Loving conversations over the back of the pew about life in general are very important for the life of a congregation. Our English word "gossip" comes from the Old English "godsibb," meaning a god-relation such as a godfather or godmother. It came to refer to the personal conversations that close family and friends share.[3] We need to hold onto the original meaning of the word even as we resist its dark side.[4]

Author Kathleen Norris calls this "holy gossip":

> I love the part in our Presbyterian service when, before prayer, we share joys and concerns. We hear about somebody's grandkids visiting from Spokane or the birth of a great-grandchild. We also hear about someone losing a job or going into surgery. That's when the gossips get busy after church and call around. They get in touch with friends, neighbors, and relatives—does he really want to see people? Or is he too tired? Should I drop in today? That is a good use of gossip.[5]

Even if you don't like the terminology "holy gossip," I encourage you to tell your people that loving small talk is not only acceptable, it is necessary for our churches to thrive. The difference between careless and loving small talk, as we've seen all along, is found in the state of our hearts. What is the intention and purpose of our small talk? Is it idle or loving?

Does your church have unhurried time for fellowship together? If not, put it on the calendar now.

5. Agree to Bear With, Not Bite, One Another

Surprise! The church is made up of sinners. Redeemed sinners who are being sanctified, but sinners just the same. And no two sinners are alike. We are not only fallen but filled with natural differences. Therefore, church life requires forbearance. The Bible's instructions are for us to "*bear with each other* and forgive whatever grievances [we] may have against one another. [We are to] forgive as the Lord forgave [us]" (Col. 3:13). To do the opposite will bring destruction.

Paul writes,

> You, my brothers, were called to be free [the gospel frees us!]. But do not use your freedom to indulge the sinful nature; rather, serve one another in love [bear with one another]. The entire law is summed up in a single command: "Love your neighbor as yourself." If you keep on *biting* and devouring each other, watch out or you will be destroyed by each other. (Gal. 5:13–15)

We need to agree in advance to bear with each other and not to bite one another. Some churches are including a "no gossip" commitment in their church-membership covenants. That's a good idea, as long as there is good teaching about what is gossip and what is not. For example, Harvest Bible Chapel in the Chicago area asks all new members to make this commitment: "To maintain unity in fellowship, I will neither criticize nor listen to criticism concerning any member of this body and will, when personally offended, speak directly and lovingly with those involved."[6]

Of course, living out these agreements is the key. "Charlotte" recently attended a pool party at the "Barnes'" house. At the party "Madeline" expressed her displeasure at several things going on at church, including how the elders ignored a couple who were having trouble in their marriage, how a staff pastor abruptly called them and only seemed to care about their attendance patterns and membership status, and how the children's program didn't seem to be doing well, and no one was doing anything about it. Whew! Sounds like a fun party.

Charlotte called one of the staff pastors and asked him what she should do. Pastor "Brayden" explained that the elders had not ignored the troubled couple and had repeatedly tried to help them. He also said that the children's ministry was getting attention. Brayden encouraged Charlotte to go back to Madeline.

And she did. Charlotte sent Madeline an e-mail the next week.

> I have been thinking, Madeline, about what was said at the Barnes' swimming party. Would you like me to go with you to talk to Brayden or the senior pastor and see what they can do to help you and me understand what we need in our church? Love, Charlotte[7]

Amen. *That* is living out our biblical commitments to each other.

6. Be Extra Careful with Reputations

Criticism is inevitable within the church. We will not always agree with each other, but we can decide in advance to be careful with each other when we make our criticisms. This is especially true for leadership.

In Paul's instruction manual to Timothy on how to do church, he teaches that leaders should be honored. He writes, "The elders who direct the affairs of the church well are worthy of double honor, especially those whose work is preaching and teaching. For the Scripture says, 'Do not muzzle the ox while it is treading out the grain,' and 'The worker deserves his wages'" (1 Tim. 5:17–18). (I'm not sure I like being called Pastor Ox, but the Lord has definitely blessed me with a church that honors me and cares for my family.)

This double honor that Paul speaks of extends to carefulness with people's reputations:

> Do not entertain an accusation against an elder unless it is brought by two or three witnesses. Those who sin are to be rebuked publicly, so that the others may take warning. I charge you, in the sight of God and Christ Jesus and the elect angels, to keep these instructions without partiality, and to do nothing out of favoritism. (1 Tim. 5:19–21)

Clearly, the church must hold its leaders accountable. We are not above accusation; on the contrary, we are held to a higher standard than those in our congregations. We must be rebuked publicly if we have fallen into unrepentant, disqualifying sin or heresy. We must be rebuked without favoritism. I tell my people, "Don't fail to rebuke me because you like me. Because you love me and love God, rebuke me if necessary."

The standard for presenting accusatory evidence is also higher. Having "two or three witnesses" will rule out gossip. The congregation should not listen to someone (especially an anonymous someone) who wants to share bad news behind a church leader's back instead of bringing it out into the open. We should not allow this for anyone in the church, but because many pastors' livelihoods and families depend upon the pastor's reputation, we must take special care. Church leaders can be destroyed by gossip. One of my pastor friends is hanging on to his ministry by his fingernails right now because a few malcontents have started a whisper campaign.

Does your church have a biblical procedure in place for handling accusations?

7. Watch What You Say to Outsiders

If we need to be careful within the church with people's reputations, how much more should we be cautious in how we talk about our fellow church members to those outside our church?

In a meditation on David's reaction to hearing about the death of King Saul in Second Samuel 1, D.A. Carson makes this present-day application:

> When one of our leaders falls, conduct yourself in such a way as not to give strength to the opposition.
>
> When a minister of the Gospel is caught embezzling funds or having an affair, then certainly the biblical principle for discipline must be brought to bear immediately. If the law has been broken, the civil authorities must be contacted. If families have been damaged, there may be a great deal of pastoral work to be done. But understand well that many unbelievers will be gleefully rubbing their hands and saying, "See? What can you expect? All this religious stuff is so hypocritical and phony." Thus Christ is despised and the credibility of Christian witnesses diminished. Christians must restrain their tongues, watch what they say, and be especially careful about saying anything unnecessary to unbelievers. This is a time for mourning, not gossip. "Tell it not in Gath . . ."[8]

Dr. Carson is right. Unbelievers don't need ammunition for their unbelief. We should be careful here and should also instruct our followers to guard their tongues around outsiders.

At the same time, as leaders, we also need to watch what we

say about our followers. It is easy for pastors to fall into complaining not just with unbelievers but with other shepherds about our sheep. How many pastor-to-pastor conversations have fallen into gripe sessions and gossip? What motivates our hearts when we talk to outsiders about our inside problems?

8. Open Channels for Airing Concerns

The flip side to the last two points is that leaders must create and sustain open channels of communication in the church for those who have concerns. Sometimes when there is gossip within a church, it is actually the leaders' fault. Those who are gossiping should not be doing it, but gossip flourishes when there is an oppressive regime and a tyrannical atmosphere of silence.

When was the last time you asked for constructive feedback? Paul told Timothy, "The Lord's servant must not quarrel; instead, he must be kind to everyone, able to teach, not resentful" (2 Tim. 2:24). That does not mean that a good church leader will agree with all the criticisms he receives or will budge on orthodoxy, but he will humble himself to solicit critique.

Being approachable is easier said than done. I know I have failed to listen more than I have succeeded, but I often quote Proverbs 27:6 to my people: "Wounds from a friend can be trusted, but an enemy multiplies kisses." Hurt me, friend, if I need it. That is love.

9. Call Each Other Out

The apostle John had a problem with a church he cared about. The church was being hijacked by a Church Boss named Diotrephes:

> I wrote to the church, but Diotrephes, who loves to be first, will have nothing to do with us. So if I come, I will call atten-

tion to what he is doing, gossiping maliciously about us. Not satisfied with that, he refuses to welcome the brothers. He also stops those who want to do so and puts them out of the church. (3 John 9–10)

Self-important Diotrephes had tried to take over the church, and he was not even allowing missionaries to visit. Worse, he was gossiping maliciously about John. If you think being godly will protect you from gossip, forget about it. You can be John the apostle, and people will still gossip about you.

So John called Diotrephes out. He named the name, and he named the sin. He said, "I will call attention to what he is doing." John was not gossiping about Diotrephes, even though he was bearing bad news about him. He was holding Diotrephes accountable. If Diotrephes refused to repent, I am certain John was forced to discipline him.

Proverbs says, "Without wood a fire goes out; without gossip a quarrel dies down" (26:20). The word "gossip" in this verse is actually a person, not a kind of talk. A better translation might be, "Without *a gossiper* a quarrel dies down." The King James Version says, "Where there is no talebearer, the strife ceaseth."

We need to call each other out when we see church members maliciously gossiping and, as a last resort, be willing to exercise church discipline. Sometimes unity is preserved by excluding from the fellowship someone who causes dissension. (Remember how much God hates disunity!) It might seem counterintuitive to ask someone to leave, but unity is sometimes preserved by cutting out a part of the body that will not function as part of the unit.

It's important to note that discipline for gossip can be done poorly. One of my friends belonged to a church that once excommunicated a member for gossip. The problem was, the proceedings were just as gossipy as the charges. Don't discipline your people if you are not willing to do it right. Nevertheless, it is loving for us to hold each other accountable for godly living.

Writer Chris Bruce adds to this principle in reference to Third John:

> Notice what John doesn't say. He doesn't tell us what the gossip is about. That's important because even as he brings the problem out into the open, we hear nothing about the actual accusation Diotrephes leveled against John. It's a good example of how to take action against someone who's gossiping without furthering the gossip itself.[9]

As far as you can help it, do not allow a hearing for gossip, even as you call someone out for bearing bad news behind another person's back.

10. Remember the Gospel

Our church's unofficial motto is, "The main thing is to keep the main thing the main thing, and the main thing is the gospel of Jesus Christ." Leaders have the responsibility to keep the gospel central to the life of the local church.

We have seen throughout this book how the gospel defeats gossip. As individuals, the gospel empowers us to resist gossip's lure and gives us the ability to love instead. The gospel also covers us with grace when we have failed. Corporately, the gospel is what binds us together in unity. God tells his church,

> Be completely humble and gentle; be patient, bearing with one another in love. Make every effort to keep the unity of the Spirit through the bond of peace. There is one body and one Spirit—just

as you were called to one hope when you were called—one Lord, one faith, one baptism; one God and Father of all, who is over all and through all and in all. (Eph. 4:2–6)

The good news of Jesus Christ brings us together, with all our sin and all our differences, and it holds us together. Because of Christ's cross and His empty tomb, we now have the Lord Jesus in common, and that is everything!

We have unity in the gospel, so we are called to preserve it.

Is It Possible?

Chris Bruce paints an insightful word picture of what can happen when church leaders do their job:

> Gossip is a serious problem for churches, but it doesn't have to be. If, as James says, the tongue can light a great fire, then we might think of the church as a tree. On the one hand, we can neglect to water the tree, and stand by with a hose to put out fires that threaten its dry and brittle branches. But the much better course is to continually keep the tree watered and moist with the truth of the Gospel and the Bible's teaching on godly speech. A tree like that, even when it encounters the flame, will not easily catch fire. A tree like that will grow and bear much fruit.[10]

Fellow leader, when I read that, I think of Smokey the Bear pointing his finger at you and me and saying, "Only you can prevent forest fires." Will we do what is needed to care for the church so that it prospers? Will our churches be bombs that threaten to blow up with every spark of gossip, or will they be healthy, flame-retardant and gossip-resistant?

Is It Worth It?

Preserving unity is a lot of work. Being a church leader in times of conflict is an especially tiring, thankless job. But we know that God loves unity among the brothers. We know that He does not want our churches to be dry, stale and lifeless. He wants them to be gooey with holy unity and refreshingly green and verdant with life. Unity will attract, not repel, a watching world. Our Lord told us, "By this will all men know that you are my disciples, if you have love for one another" (John 13:35 NASB). Unity is absolutely worth the effort!

Discussion Questions for Church Leadership Teams

1. Read Psalm 133 and Proverbs 6:16–19 and then share your observations. What does God think about brotherly unity? How highly does our Lord value unity among brothers?

2. How much of a problem is gossip in our local churches? On a scale of one (gossip-resistant) to ten (Corinth-level), how would you rate the gossip saturation? Why do you say that?

3. When was the last time you prayed against gossip as a leadership team or church family? How can you work that into your programming in the near future?

4. In what ways can your team be spiritual thermostats instead of thermometers? Do you take the qualifications for leadership seriously, especially the ones about the tongue? What can you do to improve your screening process?

5. What and when have you taught the people of your church about gossip? Can your members recognize gossip when it is happening? Are they equipped to resist it? Is it time for a refresher course?

6. How can you encourage loving small talk? Does your church or ministry have enough unhurried time for fellowship together?

7. Read Colossians 3:12–17 and Galatians 5:13–15 and contrast the passages. Does your church have a commitment to bearing with others and not "biting and devouring" them? Is that commitment formal or informal? If informal, do you need to formalize it in some way?

8. How are you treating people's reputations with care, both inside and outside the church? Does your church have a biblical procedure in place for carefully evaluating accusations against leadership (see 1 Tim. 5:17–21)? Do you have open channels for people to air their concerns? What can you do to improve in this area?

9. Read Third John 9–10. Is there a Diotrephes among your church body right now? Is there someone who needs to be called out for malicious gossip? If so, what should be your plan? If not, how can you encourage your church family to see God's blessing in your unity?

10. Is your church gospel-centered? How can your team lead your church deeper into the good of the good news?

Notes

Chapter 1: What, Exactly, Is Gossip?

1. 1. Robert H. O'Connell in Willem A. VanGemeren, ed., "4269 להם" *New International Dictionary of Old Testament Theology and Exegesis* (NIDOTTE), (Grand Rapids: Zondervan, 1997), 2:766–67; see also P.J.J.S. Els in O'Connell, "4260 להט" NIDOTTE, 2:760; Bruce K. Waltke, *The Book of Proverbs: Chapters 15–31, New International Commentary on the New Testament* (NICOT) (Grand Rapids: Eerdmans, 2005), 74; Derek Kidner, *Proverbs, Tyndale Old Testament Commentary* (TOTC), 15 (Downers Grove, IL: Inter-Varsity Press, 1971), 128.

Chapter 2: Why Do We Gossip?

1. I am grateful to my doctoral advisor, Winston Smith, for sharpening my thinking with this insight.
2. Lynette is not this woman's real name, but her story is real. I am thankful for all the people who shared their stories with me, especially those who humbly admitted to sinful gossiping! Each time a new fictional name appears throughout the book, I will note its first use with quotation marks.

3. Anonymous e-mail message to author, April 21, 2010.
4. Ibid.
5. I learned this illustration from members of the faculty of the Christian Counseling and Educational Foundation.
6. Anonymous e-mail message to author, April 21, 2010.

Chapter 3: A Gallery of Gossips

1. Joe Raposo and Jeffrey Moss, *The Sesame Street Song Book* (New York: Simon & Schuster, 1971), 43–45.
2. Anonymous e-mail message to author, May 19, 2011.
3. O'Connell, "8215 רָכִיל" NIDOTTE, 3:1114–15. Scholars connect the Hebrew word *rakil* (gossip) with the similar word *ragal*, "to go about" or "to make traveled, explored, spied out, exposed, defamed." See also The Brown-Driver-Briggs Hebrew and English Lexicon (BDB), 920 and 940.
4. Anonymous e-mail message to author, March 30, 2010.
5. Anonymous e-mail message to author, May 19, 2011.
6. Gary V. Smith in O'Connell, ed., "8087 רנן" NIDOTTE, 3:1053.
7. Anonymous personal correspondence to author, summer of 2011.
8. Anonymous comment on Matt Mitchell, "Gossip Game #3—The Big Mo," *Hot Orthodoxy*, May 19, 2011, http://matt-mitchell.blogspot.com/2011/05/gossip-game-3-big-mo.html?showComment=1305824149847#c2572334793404717719 (accessed August 9, 2011)

Chapter 4: Believing the Best

1. Timothy Keller and David Powlison, "Should You Pass on Bad Reports?" in Justin Taylor, "Keller and Powlison: Should You Pass on Bad Reports?" *Between Two Worlds*, August 4, 2008, http://thegospelcoalition.org/blogs/justintaylor/2008/08/04/keller-and-powlison-should-you-pass-on/ (accessed June 30, 2011).
2. Ken Sande, "Judging Others: The Danger of Playing God," *Journal of Biblical Counseling* 21, no. 1 (Fall 2002): 12. This article is the best place to start learning how to counter sinful judging with charitable judgments.
3. Anonymous e-mail message to author, August 31, 2010.
4. Sande, "Judging Others," 17.

Chapter 5: Instead of Gossip: Speaking

1. Peter T. O'Brien, *The Letter to the Ephesians* (Grand Rapids: Eerdmans, 1999), 344.
2. Abraham Lincoln in Waltke, *The Book of Proverbs: Chapters 15–31* in NICOT, 64.
3. Anonymous personal correspondence to author, summer 2011.
4. Sam Crabtree, *Practicing Affirmation: God-Centered Praise of Those Who Are Not God* (Wheaton: Crossway, 2011), 149–60.
5. Amy Carmichael in Raymond C. Ortlund, Jr., "Gossip," *Christ Is Deeper Still*, May 18, 2009, http://thegospelcoalition.org/blogs/rayortlund/2009/05/18/gossip/ (accessed July 12, 2011).

Chapter 6: Instead of Gossip: Listening

1. Joseph M. Stowell, *The Weight of Your Words: Measuring the*

Impact of What You Say (Chicago: Moody, 1998), 138.
2. Diana Kleyn, *Bearing Fruit: Stories about Godliness for Children* (Grand Rapids: Reformation Heritage, 2007), 136–37.
3. Anonymous e-mail message to author, August 19, 2011.

Chapter 7: Responding in Faith

1. After you study Psalm 140 in this chapter, go deeper by analyzing Psalms 35, 37, 55, 59 and 69 for more wisdom on surviving attacks with verbal weapons.
2. William Shakespeare, *Othello*, 3.3.
3. Anonymous personal correspondence to author, summer 2011.
4. Ibid.
5. I am indebted to Douglas Wilson and John Piper for these insights. Douglas Wilson, "Not Wanting to Look Bad," *Blog and Mablog*, February 5, 2011, http://dougwils.com/index.php?option=com_content&view=article&id=8410:not-wanting-to-look-bad&catid=43:exhortation (accessed October 18, 2011). The language of "unjustly bad" came from John Piper, "What If Your Reputation Is Unjustly Bad?" *Desiring God*, February 19, 2011, http://www.desiringgod.org/blog/posts/what-if-your-reputation-is-unjustly-bad (accessed October 18, 2011).

Chapter 8: Responding in Love

1. Anonymous e-mail message to author, August 17, 2011.

Chapter 9: Regretting Gossip

1. Lori Palatnik with Bob Burg, *Gossip: Ten Pathways to Eliminate It from Your Life and Transform Your Soul* (Deerfield

Beach, FL: Simcha, 2002), 3.
2. Anonymous e-mail message to author, April 21, 2010.
3. Rabbi Joseph Telushkin, *Words that Hurt, Words that Heal: How to Choose Words Wisely and Well* (New York: Quill, 1998), 3.
4. Palatnik with Burg, *Gossip*, 116.
5. Ibid.

Bonus Chapter for Church Leaders: Cultivating a Gossip-resistant Church

1. William D. Mounce, *Word Biblical Commentary*, vol. 46, *Pastoral Epistles* (Nashville: Thomas Nelson, 2000), 199.
2. C.J. Mahaney and David Powlison, "Is Small Talk Worthless?" *C.J.'s View from the Cheap Seats*, January 19, 2011, http://www.sovereigngraceministries.org/blogs/cj-mahaney/post/Is-Small-Talk-Worthless.aspx (accessed September 3, 2011).
3. *The Oxford English Dictionary*, 3rd ed., s.v. "gossip," www.oed.com/viewdictionaryentry/Entry/80197 (accessed February 1, 2011).
4. For more on this idea, see my article "Is It Ok to Use the Word 'Gossip' to Describe Something Good?' *Hot Orthodoxy*, April 16, 2013, www.matt-mitchell.blogspot.com/2013/04/is-it-ok-to-use-word-gossip-to-describe.html.
5. Kathleen Norris, interview by Mark Galli and David Goetz, "Amazing Grace-Filled Gossip: An Interview with Author Kathleen Norris," *Leadership Journal* 20, no. 1 (Winter 1999): 56–61, http://www.christianitytoday.com/le/1999/winter/9l1056.html (accessed July 26, 2011).

6. The membership commitments of Harvest Bible Chapel can be seen on their website at http://www.harvestbiblechapel.org/content.aspx?site_id=10780&content_id=300235 (accessed May 21, 2013).
7. Anonymous e-mail message to author, August 19, 2011.
8. D.A. Carson, "2 Samuel 1; 1 Corinthians 12; Ezekiel 10; Psalm 49," *For the Love of God*, September 7, 2010, http://thegospelcoalition.org/blogs/loveofgod/2010/09/07/2-samuel-1-1-corinthians-12-ezekiel-10-psalm-49/ (accessed September 3, 2011).
9. Chris Bruce, "What to Do About 'He Said, She Said' in the Church," *9Marks: Building Healthy Churches*, August 2006, http://www.alliancenet.org/CC/article/0,,PTID314526_CHID598014_CIID2238742,00.html, (accessed September 3, 2011).
10. Ibid.

Going Deeper

Recommended Reading for Resisting Gossip

I love to recommend good books to people! Here is a chapter-by-chapter list of some of the best books I read while writing *Resisting Gossip*. The wisdom of these books shaped and sharpened my thinking on how to win the war of the wagging tongue.

If you are also wondering what *not to read*, visit my website, www.matt-mitchell.blogspot.com, where I critique books that address the problem of gossip.

Chapter 1: What, Exactly, Is Gossip?

Stop the Runaway Conversation: Take Control Over Gossip and Criticism
by Dr. Michael D. Sedler (Chosen, 2001).

This is the only other full-length book on gossip, besides the one you are reading, that I can recommend. Sedler emphasizes how defiled we can become by giving in to sinful gossip and offers wisdom on how to avoid listening to evil reports.

Respectable Sins: Confronting the Sins We Tolerate
by Jerry Bridges (NavPress, 2007).

Ever notice how we can point our fingers at the sins of society while overlooking our own? Bridges earmarks gossip as a sin that we too easily accept in our circles and in ourselves.

Chapter 2: Why Do We Gossip?

The God Who Is There: Finding Your Place in God's Story
by D.A. Carson (Baker, 2010).

We are living inside the greatest story ever told. D.A. Carson introduces us to who God really is by unpacking the biblical storyline.

The Weight of Your Words: Measuring the Impact of What You Say
by Joseph M. Stowell (Moody, 1998).

Dr. Stowell shows readers how powerful words can really be and reminds us from where they come. He describes malicious gossip and slander as "catastrophic cousins" and yet gives a hope-filled roadmap to help us find our way out of the problem.

War of Words: Getting to the Heart of Your Communication Struggles
by Paul David Tripp (P&R, 2001).

Tripp tells the story of the battle of words going on around us and inside us. Whose agenda are we following—God's or Satan's? This war can be won through the gospel of Jesus Christ.

Chapter 3: A Gallery of Gossips

Proverbs: An Introduction & Commentary
by Derek Kidner (InterVarsity Press, 1984).

Meet the people in the neighborhood of Proverbs! Kidner's comments are always concise, precise and incisive.

When People Are Big and God Is Small: Overcoming Peer Pressure, Codependency, and the Fear of Man
by Edward T. Welch (P&R, 1997).

The fear of man will often snare us into gossip (see Prov. 29:25). Welch explains how the holy fear of God dispels our unhealthy fear of other people.

The Purifying Power of Living by Faith in Future Grace
by John Piper (Multnomah, 2005).

Sin promises what it cannot and will not deliver. Piper shows how we are sanctified by believing the superior promises of God.

Chapter 4: Believing the Best

Judging Others: The Danger of Playing God
by Ken Sande (Peacemaker Ministries, 2001).

Building upon Jonathan Edwards' classic work *Charity and Its Fruits,* Ken Sande's popular journal article has been released as a pocket-sized booklet aimed at helping believers to counter sinful judging with charitable judgments.

Who Are You to Judge? The Dangers of Judging and Legalism
by Dave Swavely (P&R, 2005).

Swavely cuts through our current cultural fog with biblical definitions of judging and legalism, and he teaches us how to "cross-examine" our judgments about other people.

Chapter 5: Instead of Gossip: Speaking

How People Change
by Timothy S. Lane and Paul David Tripp
(New Growth, 2008).

How do Christians change? Lane and Tripp explain the biblical principles of personal transformation in a simple, readable, memorable way. We don't have to be the way we used to be. We can live differently now because of Christ.

Practicing Affirmation: God-Centered Praise of Those Who Are Not God
by Sam Crabtree (Crossway, 2011).

Crabtree not only explains why we should praise people but writes about how to do so in a way that glorifies God. *Practic-*

ing Affirmation gives the other side of the "coin" that you hold in your hands—what to say rather than what not to say—and the last chapter, "100 Affirmation Ideas for Those Who Feel Stuck," is worth the proverbial price of the book.

Chapter 6: Instead of Gossip: Listening

A Praying Life: Connecting with God in a Distracting World
by Paul E. Miller (NavPress, 2009).

We need wisdom and grace when we find ourselves in gossip situations. Miller expertly teaches us how to weave prayer into the fabric of our everyday lives.

Shame Interrupted: How God Lifts the Pain of Worthlessness and Rejection
by Edward T. Welch (New Growth, 2012).

Gossip tells a shame-filled story about someone else. Welch tells the biblical counter-story of God covering, absorbing and undoing our shame through Jesus Christ.

Chapter 7: Responding in Faith

When God Weeps: Why Our Sufferings Matter to the Almighty
by Joni Eareckson Tada and Steven Estes (Zondervan, 2000).

It hurts to be the victim of gossip. *When God Weeps* is the best book I've ever read about the problem of pain, and it is written by someone who knows what it is like to suffer. Tada and Estes show us how God is sovereign over our suffering and, at the same time, cares deeply about our pain.

The Peacemaker: A Biblical Guide to Resolving Personal Conflict
by Ken Sande (Baker, 2004).

Ken Sande offers a comprehensive overview of the personal

peacemaking process, and he says that the first step in this process is to focus on glorifying God. With each conflict we find ourselves in, God provides opportunities for us to trust in Him and to do good.

Chapter 8: Responding in Love

Love in Hard Places
by D.A. Carson (Crossway, 2002).

Love my enemy?! Building on his previous work, T*he Difficult Doctrine of the Love of God*, Carson offers rich wisdom about love, forgiveness and the gospel applied to the hard cases we encounter in real life.

Love Walked Among Us: Learning to Love Like Jesus
by Paul E. Miller (NavPress, 2001).

Few books have opened my eyes to who Jesus is and how He loves people as much as *Love Walked Among Us* has. Miller paints both a vivid portrait of the Jesus we find in the Gospels and a compelling picture of how, by faith, we can follow Christ's divine example in our day-to-day relationships.

Unpacking Forgiveness: Biblical Answers for Complex Questions and Deep Wounds
by Chris Brauns (Crossway, 2008).

Being the victim of gossip raises a cornucopia of questions: What is forgiveness? Should I just get over what happened? How can I conquer bitterness? How can I stop thinking about it? Brauns unpacks and then answers each question with biblical clarity and practical counsel for forgiving those who have sinned against us.

Chapter 9: Regretting Gossip

The Great Work of the Gospel: How We Experience God's Grace
by John Ensor (Crossway, 2006).

We cannot really understand how great God's grace is until we begin to grasp how sinful we have been. John Ensor richly surveys the glory of the gospel of Jesus Christ and helps us to feel the tremendous relief of being truly forgiven.

Forgiveness: "I Just Can't Forgive Myself!"
by Robert D. Jones (P&R, 2000).

Sometimes our regrets can overpower us. In this helpful booklet Jones argues against the mistaken concept of "self-forgiveness" while offering the biblical alternative of grasping God's forgiveness in Christ.

The Last Enemy: Preparing to Win the Fight of Your Life
by Michael E. Wittmer (Discovery House, 2012).

This is a book about preparing for death—not a happy subject but one that we all need to ponder. Wittmer helps us to get ready, through the good news of Jesus, for the enemy that comes after each of us. Along the way, he teaches us biblical principles for living our lives now with no regrets.

Bonus Chapter for Church Leaders: Cultivating a Gossip-resistant Church

The Peacemaking Pastor: A Biblical Guide to Resolving Church Conflict
by Alfred Poirier (Baker, 2006).

Pastor Poirier doesn't just teach how to resolve conflict, but he also shows how we can lead our churches to pursue a culture of peace. From his illustrations and personal stories, it is clear that he practices what he preaches.

How To Treat a Staff Infection: Resolving Problems in Your Church or Ministry Team
by Craig and Carolyn Williford (Baker, 2007).

Among a long list of maladies from which your church or ministry team might be suffering, the Willifords list "Flaccidity of the Lips," with the symptoms being that "gossip is passed off as 'prayer requests.'" They give practical suggestions for resolving this problem that start with self-examination.

The Cross and Christian Ministry: Leadership Lessons from 1 Corinthians
by D.A. Carson (Baker, 2004).

Carson reminds us that the main thing in church leadership is to keep the main thing the main thing. This is a book to read and then re-read regularly.

Acknowledgments

I am a grateful man because I am a blessed man.

I am grateful for my family. Thank you, Heather Joy, for telling me, "You can, should and *will* get this project done!" Thank you, Robin, Andrew, Peter and Isaac, for listening to your dad go on and on about gossip at the dinner table. You know more about resisting gossip than any other children I know. Thank you, Mom and Dad Mitchell, for encouraging me all my life in whatever strange ideas I got into my head—including the idea of writing a book on gossip. Thank you, extended family, for asking me, "How's the project coming?" and for actually wanting to hear the answer!

I am grateful for Lanse Evangelical Free Church. Thank you, LEFC elders, for talking me out of a sabbatical—that really wouldn't have worked as well as the writing weeks did. Thank you, LEFC congregation, for listening to many more sermons on gossip than any local church ever should have to. Thank you, Pastoral Prayer Team, for lifting up this project time after time. Thank you, Stacey Fisch, Holly Crumrine and Marilynn Kristofits, for holding down the fort in the office when I was so preoccupied. Thank you, Nesta Kephart, for encouraging me early on to "stay positive" in the book and to offer the reader hope in every chapter—that significantly shaped the whole project. Thank you, Rachel Confer, for a special gift at just the right moment.

I am grateful for our family of churches, the EFCA (Evangelical Free Church of America). Thank you, "Super Jeff" Powell and the Allegheny District pastors, for supporting me throughout this process. Thank you, Diane McDougall, for giving me so many opportunities to learn the craft of writing as a part of *EFCA Today*. Thank you, Robert Jones, for introducing me to CCEF (Christian Counseling & Educational Foundation).

I am grateful for the CCEF and WTS (Westminster Theological Seminary) faculty and staff. Thank you, Ed Welch, for recommending that I write a book for ordinary Christians (not just for church leaders) and for saying, "I'd want to read it." Thank you, Winston Smith, Mike Emlet, David Powlison and Tim Lane, for the quality of counseling education you offer us CCEF students. I would sit under your training all over again.

I am grateful for the folks who helped to get this book actually published. Thank you, Aunt Susie, Emily Chase, Chris Brauns and Gary Friesen, for your counsel on crafting the proposal and on connecting with publishers. Thank you, Laurel Eriksen, Nate Weatherly, Donnie Rosie and Schenley Pilgram, for making my wordy blog something nice to look at. Thank you, Gary Foster, for being an excellent matchmaker of an agent. Thank you, CLC Ministries, especially Dave Almack, for taking a chance on a rookie author, and Tracey Lewis-Giggetts, for putting up with my fussiness and taking the manuscript to the next level.

I am grateful for my "critical readers" who read the manuscript and gave me valuable input. Thank you, Chris Brauns, Kim Cone, Jaroslav and Natalija Elijas, Stacey Fisch, Rachel Joy, Mark Lauterbach, Dan and Jen Ledford, Diane McDougall, Tim McIntosh, Natasha Miller, Elizabeth Nelson, Jani Ortlund, Jennifer Petoske, Marty Schoenleber, Susan Stallings (and your guinea-pig small group!), Dennis Wadsworth, Bruce and Donna Weatherly and Kipp Wilson. Clarence was right when he told George Bailey that no man is a failure who has friends.

I am grateful for "Lynnette" and all the others who trusted me with your stories—especially those who admitted to gossiping. You were brave, and others will be helped.

I am especially grateful for my King and Rescuer, the Lord Jesus Christ. May You and Your Father get all the glory.

About the Author

Matt Mitchell is Heather's hubby and daddy to Robin, Andrew, Peter and Isaac. He has pastored Lanse Evangelical Free Church [www.lansefree.org], a 120-year-old rural church parked along Interstate 80, since 1998. The Mitchells live in the woods of Central Pennsylvania with a flock of free-range chickens. They love to read books, play games and go for long hikes.

A graduate of Moody Bible Institute and Trinity Evangelical Divinity School, Pastor Matt received his doctorate in biblical counseling from Westminster Theological Seminary in 2012. Matt is active in his family of churches, the Evangelical Free Church of America [www.efca.org] and is the book review coordinator for *EFCA Today* [www.efcatoday.org]. He loves getting to talk about Jesus at conferences, seminars, retreats and workshops.

Matt writes a blog about passionate truth called *Hot Orthodoxy*, where he posts his thoughts on pastoral ministry and biblical counseling, book reviews and sermon manuscripts, links to helpful and humorous places, glimpses into family life and personal reflections along the journey of following the Lord Jesus Christ with both head and heart.

The most amazing thing about Matt is that Jesus loves him even though he doesn't deserve it, and that gives Matt the greatest joy and the greatest message to share with others. He loves to "gossip" the gospel of grace. *Resisting Gossip* is his first book.

Join the conversation!
Find more resources for resisting gossip at
www.matt-mitchell.blogspot.com

This book was produced by CLC Publications. We hope it has been life-changing and has given you a fresh experience of God through the work of the Holy Spirit. CLC Publications is an outreach of CLC Ministries International, a global literature mission with work in over fifty countries. If you would like to know more about us or are interested in opportunities to serve with a faith mission, we invite you to contact us at:

CLC Ministries International
PO Box 1449
Fort Washington, PA 19034

E-mail: mail@clcusa.org
Website: www.clcpublications.com

DO YOU LOVE GOOD CHRISTIAN BOOKS?
Do you have a heart for worldwide missions?

You can receive a FREE subscription to
CLC's newsletter on global literature missions
Order by e-mail at:
clcworld@clcusa.org
or mail your request to:
**PO Box 1449
Fort Washington, PA 19034**